TRUTH FOR LIFE®

THE BIBLE-TEACHING MINISTRY OF **ALISTAIR BEGG**

The mission of Truth For Life is to teach the Bible with clarity and relevance so that unbelievers will be converted, believers will be established, and local churches will be strengthened.

Daily Program

Each day, Truth For Life distributes the Bible teaching of Alistair Begg across the U.S. and in several locations outside of the U.S. through 1,800 radio outlets. To find a radio station near you, visit **truthforlife.org/stationfinder**.

Free Teaching

The daily program, and Truth For Life's entire teaching archive of over 2,000 Bible-teaching messages, can be accessed for free online and through Truth For Life's full-feature mobile app. Download the free mobile app at **truthforlife.org/app** and listen free online at **truthforlife.org**.

At-Cost Resources

Books and full-length teaching from Alistair Begg on CD, DVD, and USB are available for purchase at cost, with no markup. Visit **truthforlife.org/store**.

Where to Begin?

If you're new to Truth For Life and would like to know where to begin listening and learning, find starting point suggestions at **truthforlife. org/firststep**. For a full list of ways to connect with Truth For Life, visit **truthforlife.org/subscribe**.

Contact Truth For Life

P.O. Box 398000 Cleveland, Ohio 44139
phone 1 (888) 588-7884   **email** letters@truthforlife.org
 /truthforlife   @truthforlife   truthforlife.org

"'All our yesterdays," according to Shakespeare's Macbeth, 'have lighted fools the way to dusty death'. Not so, writes Tim Chester—instead we hear the voices of the past telling of the mighty works of God and helping us to fix our eyes on Jesus. Every page of this book is an opportunity to sit and learn at the feet of saints of old as Chester brilliantly guides us from the foot of the cross to the empty tomb. In *An Ocean of Grace* we discover one blessing after another."

ALISTAIR BEGG, Bible Teacher, Truth For Life;
Senior Pastor, Parkside Church, Cleveland, Ohio

"This collection of prayers from the past is a gift that stands out in a world of quick and casual words. Tim Chester has provided a profoundly beautiful way to help lead the church in prayer during the Lenten season. The prayers of these men and women are not only saturated with biblical truth; they are also shaped with imagination that awakens us and love for Jesus that pierces our hearts."

KATHLEEN NIELSON, Author; Speaker

"Lent is a great time to slow down and take time to think again about the events of the first Easter. This book helps us to do just that. After a typically clear and thoughtful introduction by Tim Chester, each day there is a treasure from a great Christian writer of the past. Each of these prayers, poems and mediations makes us slow down and take time as we get to grips with the richness of the language and the depth of thought, and allow these writers of old to bring us fresh insights into the wonders of the gospel."

CLARE HEATH-WHYTE, Author, *Old Wives' Tales*

TIM CHESTER

An Ocean of Grace

thegoodbook
COMPANY

An Ocean of Grace
© Tim Chester, 2021

Published by:
The Good Book Company

thegoodbook.com | thegoodbook.co.uk
thegoodbook.com.au | thegoodbook.co.nz | thegoodbook.co.in

Unless indicated, all Scripture references are taken from the Holy Bible, New International Version. Copyright © 2011 Biblica, Inc. Used by permission.

Tim Chester has asserted his right under the Copyright, Designs and Patents Act 1988 to be identified as author of this work.

ISBN: 9781784985790 | Printed in Turkey

Design by André Parker

CONTENTS

INTRODUCTION

A GREAT CLOUD OF WITNESSES

*"Therefore, since we are surrounded by such a great cloud of
witnesses, let us throw off everything that hinders and the sin
that so easily entangles. And let us run with perseverance the
race marked out for us, fixing our eyes on Jesus, the pioneer
and perfecter of faith."
(Hebrews 12 v 1-2)*

The Christian life is a long race. But we're not running on
our own.

According to Hebrews 12 v 1-2, we need to do two
things if we're to keep going as Christians and so complete
the "race" marked out for us. They're flagged up by the two
"let us" phrases. First, we're to turn away from distractions,
especially the distraction of sin ("let us throw off everything
that hinders"). Second, we're to turn instead to look at Jesus
("let us ... [fix] our eyes on Jesus"). Lent and Easter are a
great opportunity to do this with a special focus.

To help fix our gaze on Jesus, we are surrounded by "a
great cloud of witnesses". For the first readers of Hebrews,
these witnesses were the saints of the Old Testament,
whose faith in God's promises had sustained them through
troubling times and had enabled them to achieve great
things in God's name. But as readers today, we can add
names from across the pages of church history to that crowd
of cheering spectators. Two thousand years on, the cloud of

witnesses is larger than ever. This book is an opportunity to hear their voices. It contains prayers and meditations from across the centuries of church history, all with a focus on the death and resurrection of Jesus.

The key thing is that such people are "witnesses". Like the witness in a law court, they have evidence to present and in this case, their testimony concerns Jesus Christ. Their purpose is not to draw attention to themselves but to him. Their lives may inspire and their words may inform, but their true value is that they point us to Jesus.

Why should we read the words of dead Christians when we are surrounded by living ones?

First, because these people are our brothers and sisters, as much part of the community of saints as the people in your church. God worked in them and through them in the past, and he does so again when their words are heard.

Also, because it's as if these people speak with a different voice. The language which can sometimes sound strange to our ears has—for that very reason—the power to speak the truth to us with fresh vigour. The phrases we have heard a hundred times are replaced by new expressions that renew our thinking and engage our imagination.

Finally, because "sitting at the feet" of those from other times allows us to view our times from outside. These saints of old give us a perspective on ourselves—our foibles and assumptions. The emphases we miss are highlighted, and the preoccupations that distract us are put into perspective.

In editing these readings, archaic language has been removed (with the exception of poetry and hymns), while retaining the distinctive "voice" of the original author. In many cases descriptions have been turned into a prayer addressed to God or an exhortation addressed to our own souls. Some chapters are made up of selected highlights from longer passages. In every chapter the aim is to direct our hearts to the Lord Jesus Christ. I recommend reading these meditations aloud. You might like to read them through once and then reread them more slowly, responding section by section with prayers of confession and praise.

My primary aim has not been to provide new information or explain in detail the nature of Christ's work. Instead, my hope is that familiar truths will come with fresh power to capture our imaginations and captivate our hearts. Above all, let us make it our prayer that we would fix our eyes on Jesus, the pioneer and perfecter of faith.

ASH WEDNESDAY

HEAL ME

"It is Jesus' name and the faith that comes through him
that has completely healed him."
(Acts 3 v 16)

Ash Wednesday has traditionally been a day when people have reflected on their conduct and confessed their sins to God. This renews our sense of relationship with God as well as humbling our pride and exalting our Saviour. For Christians, confession need not be done with a sense of fear or doubt, for we have been saved by the name of Jesus. In the Bible a person's name often represents their authority, character or office, and this is especially true of Jesus. In Acts 3 Peter heals a lame man "in the name of Jesus Christ". In today's prayer the English Reformer Thomas Becon leads us in confessing our sin, but also reminds us of how the different names of Jesus bring comfort to wounded sinners.

Heal me, Lord, and I shall be healed.
Save me, Lord, and I shall be saved.
Oh, good Jesus, I confess my sins are great,
    but your merits are much greater.
My wounds are many and grievous;
    but you are the good Samaritan,
    full of pity and compassion;
        able to heal my wounds,
    even if they were ten thousand times greater.

I am a sinner; but you are a Saviour.
I am sick; but you are a Physician.
I am blind; but you are the Light of the world.
I am Satan's prisoner; but you are a Redeemer.
I am dead in sin; but you are the Resurrection and Life.
I am hungry; but you are the living Bread.
I am thirsty; but you are the Well of life.
I am poor; but you are the Lord of all wealth.
I am a barren tree; but you are the true and fruitful Vine.
I am a lost sheep; but you are the good Shepherd.
I am the prodigal son; but you are the gentle Father.
I am by nature a child of wrath;
    but you are by nature the Son of the living God.
I am by nature a sinful person;
    but you are by nature the righteous and innocent Man.
I am a daily offender; but you are a continual Mediator.
I am a breaker of the law; but you are the Fulfiller of the law.
I have lost my heavenly inheritance through sin;
    but you have recovered it by your death.
I have brought about my own destruction;
    but you have brought me salvation by your precious blood.

Oh, most merciful Saviour,
Though I find in myself nothing but sin,
    death and damnation,
yet I find in you grace, mercy, favour, reconciliation,
    forgiveness and everlasting life.
Take away therefore all that is mine, which is all nothing,
    and give me all that is yours, which is all good.

You are called Christ, the anointed One:
    therefore anoint me with your Holy Spirit.
You are called a Physician:
    therefore heal me according to your name.
You are called the Son of the living God:

therefore according to your power deliver me
from the devil, the world, and the flesh.
You are called the Resurrection:
therefore lift me up from the damnable state
in which I miserably lie.
You are called the Life:
therefore awaken me out of this death,
in which, through sin, I am detained.
You are called the Way:
therefore lead me from the vanities of this world,
and from the filthy pleasures of the flesh,
towards heavenly and spiritual things.
You are called the Truth:
therefore do not allow me to walk in the way of error,
but let me walk the path of truth in everything I do.
You are called the Light:
therefore put away from me the works of darkness,
that I may walk as the child of light
in all goodness, righteousness and truth.
You are called a Saviour:
therefore save me from my sins, according to your name.
You are called the Alpha and Omega—
that is, the beginning and end of all goodness:
therefore begin a good life in me,
and finish it to the glory of your blessed name.
So shall I, receiving these benefits at your merciful hand,
praise and magnify your blessed name for evermore.

Thomas Becon (c. 1512-1567)[1]

THURSDAY

I WILL CALL UPON CHRIST

"Here is a trustworthy saying that deserves full acceptance:
Christ Jesus came into the world to save sinners—of whom I
am the worst."
(1 Timothy 1 v 15)

Are you the worst sinner you know? Perhaps you are immediately starting to name all the people whom you consider worse than you. When we compare ourselves to other people, we can pretend that we're not too bad. But what about when we compare ourselves to Christ? That's what Catherine Parr, the sixth wife of King Henry VIII, does in her book *The Lamentations of a Sinner*. Comparing ourselves to Christ in this way might drive us to desperation as the extent of our sin is exposed. But when we look to Christ, we see not only our model but also our Saviour. We see the one who came into the world to save sinners. Our sin may be great, but his mercy is greater.

> *Eternal God, as a loving Father,*
> *you have heaped on me innumerable blessings;*
> *and I have heaped up many sins.*
> *I have despised that which is good, holy, pleasant*
> *and acceptable in your sight,*
> *and I have chosen that which was delicious, pleasant*
> *and acceptable in my sight.*
> *It was no surprise that I did this*

for I refused to know you and learn your ways.
I loved darkness better than light.
Indeed, darkness seemed to me to be light.
I embraced ignorance as knowledge;
    and rejected true knowledge as pointless.
I had little regard for your word
    but gave myself to the vanities and shadows of the world.
I abandoned you, in whom all is truth,
    and followed the foolish imaginations of my own heart.
You spoke many pleasant and sweet words to me,
    and I would not hear.
You called me in many ways,
    but I would not answer.

I count myself one of the most wicked
    and miserable sinners in the world
    because I have been so contrary to Christ my Saviour.
Christ was innocent and empty of all sin,
    and I wallowed in filthy sin
    and was free from no sin.
Christ was obedient to you, his Father,
even to the death of the cross,
    and I was disobedient and stubborn.
Christ was meek and humble in heart,
    and I most proud and self-serving.
Christ despised the world with all its vanities,
    and I made it my god because of its vanities.
Christ came to serve his brothers and sisters,
    and I longed to rule over them.
Christ despised worldly honour,
    and I delighted to attain it.
Christ loved the lowly and simple things of this world,
    and I esteemed the most fair and pleasant things.
Christ loved poverty,

and I loved wealth.
Christ was gentle and merciful to the poor,
  and I was hard-hearted and unkind.
Christ prayed for his enemies,
  and I hated mine.
Christ rejoiced in the conversion of sinners,
  and I was not grieved to see them revert to sin.

Shall I fall in desperation?
No, I will call upon Christ,
  the Light of the world,
    the Fountain of life,
      the relief of all careful consciences,
        the Peacemaker between God and man,
          and the only health and comfort
          of all true repentant sinners.

By his almighty power he can save me
and deliver me out of this miserable state.
For this is the life everlasting, O Lord,
  to believe you to be the true God,
  and him whom you sent, Jesus Christ.
By this faith I am assured,
and by this assurance I feel the forgiveness of my sins:
  this is what gives me confidence,
  this is what comforts me,
  this is what quenches all despair.

Catherine Parr (1512-1548)[2]

FRIDAY

ROUSE YOURSELF TO THIS END

"They will look on me, the one they have pierced, and they will mourn for him as one mourns for an only child, and grieve bitterly for him as one grieves for a firstborn son."
(Zechariah 12 v 10)

Lent is a time to reflect on the sufferings of Christ. Today the 16th-century Reformer Martin Luther gives us advice on how to do this. First, Luther says we must see our sin reflected in Christ's suffering. The depth of our sin is exposed at the cross because the cross reflects everyone's attitude to God—we reject his reign in our lives and so, when we get the opportunity, we murder our Creator. Second, our sins are exposed at the cross in the sense that the fate of the Christ is the fate our sins deserve. So Christ's sufferings bring us to recognise that we are morally bankrupt. This is an important realisation, but it's not the end point (otherwise we might despair). We must then, thirdly, move on to see God's love expressed in the Christ. God gave his Son for us, and Christ was willing to suffer for us. So as we look at the cross, we are led away from self-confidence, and then we are led towards confidence in God.

You meditate on the Passion of Christ aright
   when you become terror-stricken in heart at the sight
   and your conscience sinks in despair.
Recognise you are the one who martyred Christ,

for your sins most surely did it (Acts 2 v 36-37).
Therefore, when you see the nails piercing his hands,
*   firmly believe it is your work.*
Do you behold his crown of thorns?
*   Believe the thorns are your wicked thoughts.*
Now see that where one thorn pierces Christ,
*   more than a thousand thorns should pierce you,*
*   yes, and they should do so eternally.*
Where one nail is driven through his hands,
*   you should eternally suffer this same fate.*
Jesus commanded the women who wept for him,
*   "Do not weep for me; weep for yourselves*
*   and for your children" (Luke 23 v 28).*
In other words,
*   "Learn from my martyrdom what you deserve*
*   and how you should be rewarded."*

But, just as an awareness of sin flowed out of Christ,
*   so should we pour our sins back again onto Christ*
*   and set our conscience free.*
So then, cast your sins from yourself onto Christ,
*   believing that your sins are his wounds*
*   and that he carries them and makes satisfaction for them.*
You must rely on God's promises (e.g. Isaiah 53 v 6)
*   with all your weight,*
*   and so much more when your conscience martyrs you.*
For if you miss the opportunity to still your heart,
*   then you will never secure peace*
*   and must finally despair in doubt.*
For our sins will become too strong for us to manage
*   and they will live for ever.*
But when we fearlessly believe that our sins are laid on Christ
*   and that he has triumphed over them by his resurrection,*
then they are dead and have become as nothing.

Now if you are not able to believe,
    then you should pray to God for faith.
But rouse yourself to this end.
First, do not behold Christ's sufferings any longer,
    for they have already done their work and terrified you.
Instead, behold how full of love
    is Christ's friendly heart toward you—
    love that constrained him to bear
    the heavy load of your sin.
    In this way your heart will be sweet toward him,
        and the assurance of your faith will be strengthened.
    Then ascend higher through the heart of Christ
        to the heart of God.
    See that Christ would not have been able to love you
        if God had not willed it in eternal love.
    There you will find the good, fatherly heart of God,
        and so be drawn to the Father through Christ
    (John 3 v 16).

When your heart is established in Christ in this way,
    and you are an enemy of sin
    (out of love rather than out of fear of punishment),
        only then should Christ's sufferings
        also be an example for your life.
Then you should meditate on his sufferings in a different
way. So far we have considered Christ's Passion
    as a work of Christ that we receive;
now we may consider it
    as a work that we should imitate.
For example, if a day of sickness weighs you down,
    think how trifling that is compared with the nails of Christ.
If you must do something that is distasteful to you,
    think how Christ suffered for your sake.

Martin Luther (1483-1546)[3]

SATURDAY

THE GREAT PHYSICIAN

*"It is not the healthy who need a doctor, but those who are
ill. I have not come to call the righteous, but sinners."*
(Mark 2 v 17)

At Lent we come to Jesus confessing our sins. You might
imagine that acknowledging your sin is the very worst
way to come to God. After all, God is holy, and sin cannot exist in his pure presence. But in fact acknowledging
your sin is the *only* way to come to God. For God delights
to show mercy towards repentant hearts that come to him
in the name of Jesus. Indeed, those who acknowledge they
are sinners are exactly the sort of people Jesus came to save.
As the 19th-century preacher Charles Spurgeon reminds
us, this is how God displays the full glory of his mercy. So
admitting your need is actually the only "qualification" required for coming to Jesus.

> *Dear Saviour, we come to you as beggars,*
> *dependent on your heavenly charity.*
> *You are a Saviour,*
> *always looking out for those that need saving.*
> *And here we are, and here we come,*
> *the men and women you are looking for,*
> *   men and women needing a Saviour.*
>
> *Great Physician,*
> *we bring to you our wounds and bruises.*

The more diseased we are
and the more conscious we are of the depravity of our nature,
    of the deep-seated corruption of our hearts,
the more we feel that we are the sort of beings
    that you are seeking,
for the whole have no need of a doctor,
    but only those who are sick.

Glorious Benefactor,
we can meet you on good terms,
for we are full of poverty—as empty as we can be.
Since you would display your mercy—
    here is our sin.
Since you would show your strength—
    here is our weakness.
Since you would manifest your loving-kindness—
    here are our needs.
Since you would glorify your grace—
    here we are,
    people who can never have a shadow of a hope
    except through your grace.
For we are undeserving,
    ill-deserving,
        hell-deserving,
and if you do not magnify your grace in us
    we must perish for ever.

It is sweet to come to you in this way.
If we had to come telling you of the good in us,
we would question whether we were flattering ourselves.
But, Lord Jesus, we come just as we are.
This is how we first came to you,
and this is how we still come,
    with all our failures,
    with all our transgressions,

with all and everything that is what it ought not to be,
  we come to you.
We bless you that you receive us and our wounds,
  and by your stripes we are healed.
You receive us and our sins,
  and by your sin-bearing we are set free from sin.
You receive us and our death—even our death
  for you are the one who was dead and is alive,
    alive for evermore.

We come and lie at your feet, obedient to your call:
  "Come to me, all you who are weary and burdened,
  and I will give you rest" (Matthew 11 v 28).
Let us feel sweet rest, since we come at your invitation.
May some come that have never come until now.
May others consciously come again,
  coming to you as to a living stone,
  chosen of God and precious,
  to build our everlasting hopes upon.

May we who love you,
  love you much more.
You have been precious to us,
your name has been music to our ears,
and your love to us is inexpressibly strong.
We have felt that we would gladly die
  to increase your honour.
We have been willing to lose our reputation
  that you might be glorified,
and yet we do not always feel this passionate love.
With all the capacity that there is in us,
may we love our Lord in spirit and in truth.

Charles Spurgeon (1834-1892)[4]

The Light of Love

SUNDAY

YOUR GRACE SHINES BRIGHTEST

"God demonstrates his own love for us in this: while we were still sinners, Christ died for us."
(Romans 5 v 8)

There are a thousand ways we experience God's love every day. Each breath you breathe is his gift to you. But, as the Puritan Isaac Ambrose reminds us, God's love shines brightest at the cross. This is where we see the full extent of his love. It is revealed in the depths to which Christ was prepared to descend, leaving the glories of heaven for the shame of the cross. And it is revealed in who he endured the cross for. Anyone might love someone who is lovely, but only Jesus was prepared to die for his enemies. The glory of heaven will not be the splendour of our surroundings nor the choirs of angels. The glory of heaven will be the wounds of our Saviour.

Lord Jesus Christ,
your graces shine brightest in your bitter Passion.
Your life was a gracious life, and you are full of grace.
But as a lily seems most beautiful when among thorns,
so your graces are best seen in your sufferings.

Your humility was profound:
that the most high God,
the only begotten and eternal Son of God,
should condescend so far as to be condemned,

that you should be crucified upon a cross,
between two thieves, as if you had been their ringleader.
Oh, what humility was this!

Your patience was wonderful.
  "When they hurled their insults at him,
    he did not retaliate; when he suffered,
    he made no threats" (1 Peter 2 v 23).
Oh, what patience was this!

Your love was fervent.
  "This is love: not that we loved God,
    but that he loved us and sent his Son
    as an atoning sacrifice for our sins" (1 John 4 v 10).
Your love is the supreme example of love:
the fire that should kindle all our sparks.
Oh, what love was this!

Your mercy was abundant.
You took on yourself all our miseries and debts,
and made satisfaction for them all,
caring not what you suffered,
enacting our redemption in your own person.
We undervalue your mercy, who overvalued us;
we will not sell all to buy you, but you sold all you had
    and gave your very self to buy us.
Oh, what mercy is this!

Your meekness was great.
In all the story of your Passion,
you showed not the least passion of wrath or anger.
You suffered gently and quietly,
carried like a sheep to the butchery.
  "As a sheep before its shearers is silent,
    so he did not open his mouth" (Isaiah 53 v 7).
Oh, what meekness is this!

Your contempt for worldly glory was admirable,
saying "My kingdom is not of this world" (John 18 v 36).
You hung naked on the cross, as few kings would have done.
You had no crown for your head, except one of thorns.
You had no delicates to eat, except gall and vinegar.
You had no legacies to endow, except spiritual things.
  "Peace I leave with you; my peace I give you.
  I do not give to you as the world gives" (John 14 v 27).

Lord Jesus Christ,
you are the centre of heaven's happiness,
the wellspring that fills saints and angels.
There is as much happiness in you as happiness exists.
Whatever excellency is in heaven, it is in you.
Whatever belongs to glory is found in you.
You are all good things to all your saints in heaven:
beauty to their eyes,
  music to their ears,
    honey to their mouths,
      perfume to their nostrils,
        health to their bodies,
          joy to their souls,
            light to their understanding,
              content to their wills.
You are time without sliding,
  company without loathing,
    desire without fainting.
You are Alpha and Omega, the beginning and ending.
All the virtues, beauties and goodness
in people, animals, trees and any other creature,
are nothing but passing sparks compared to your glory.

Isaac Ambrose (1604-1664)[5]

MONDAY

AS GOD, AS MAN

"For you know the grace of our Lord Jesus Christ, that though he was rich, yet for your sake he became poor, so that you through his poverty might become rich."
(2 Corinthians 8 v 9)

When the Son of God became man, he accepted all the limitations of human life. He didn't stop being God, but he didn't use his divine power to lessen the experience of being human. He grew hungry, thirsty and tired. Jesus only used his divine power to bless others—feeding the hungry, healing the sick, raising the dead. Each one of these acts points to the cross. For at the cross Jesus died as a human being, but through his divine power his death brings life to many—as Gregory of Nazianzus, the 4th-century church father, reminds us.

Lord Jesus Christ,
we bless you and praise you
because you were baptised as man—
but you forgave sins as God.
You were tempted as man—
but you conquered as God.
Yes, you call us to be of good cheer
for you have overcome the world.

You hungered—
  but you fed thousands.
  Yes, you are the Bread that gives life;
  you are the Bread that is of heaven.
You thirsted—
  but you cried out,
  "Let anyone who is thirsty
   come to me and drink" (John 7 v 37).
  Yes, you promised that fountains would flow
  to those who believe.
You became weary—
  but you are the rest of those
  who are weary and heavy laden.
You were heavy with sleep,
  but you walked lightly over the sea.
  Yes, and you rebuked the winds,
  and made Peter light when he began to sink.
You paid tax—
  but it was out of a fish.
  Yes, and you were the King of those who demanded it.
You were called demon-possessed—
  but the demons acknowledged you,
  and you drove them out,
  seeing the prince of demons fall like lightning.
You prayed—
  but you hear prayer.
You wept—
  but you caused tears to cease.
You asked where Lazarus was laid, for you are man—
  but you raised Lazarus, for you are God.
You were sold, and very cheaply,
for it was only for thirty pieces of silver—
  but you redeemed the world,
  and did so at a great price,

for the price was your own blood.
You were led like a sheep to the slaughter—
 but you are the Shepherd of Israel,
 and now of the whole world as well.
You were silent like a lamb—
 but you are the Word.
You were bruised and wounded—
 but you heal every disease and every infirmity.
You were lifted up and nailed to the tree—
 but by the tree of life you restore us.
You were given vinegar to drink mingled with gall—
 Who? The one who turned the water into wine,
 who is the destroyer of the bitter taste of judgment,
 who is sweetness and altogether desire.
You laid down your life—
 but you had power to take it again.
 Yes, the veil is rent,
 for the doors of heaven are opened;
 the rocks are opened and the dead arise.
You died—
 but you give life,
 and by your death you have destroyed death.
You were buried—
 but you rose again;
You experienced the depths of hell—
 but from hell you rescued souls.
You ascended to heaven,
 and shall come again to judge the living and the dead.

Gregory of Nazianzus (329-390)[6]

TUESDAY

ALL LOVE AND THANKFULNESS

"We love because he first loved us."
(1 John 4 v 19)

This verse reminds us of what comes first: God's love to us. Human beings typically love something they find lovely or loving. But we were not lovely or loving when God loved us. The reasons for God's love belong solely within him—*his* eternally loving and gracious character. Our salvation did not start when we turned our lives around. It started with God and his love. But this verse also reminds us of what comes second: our love to God and other people. The experience of God's love, especially God's love seen in the cross, captures our hearts. As the Puritan Stephen Charnock reminds us, we can't go on loving the sin that led our dear Saviour to the horrors of the cross.

> *All love and thankfulness is due to you, Lord Jesus.*
> *You were numbered among transgressors*
> *that we might have a room among the blessed.*
> *Our crimes merited our sufferings,*
> *but your heart made you a sufferer for us;*
> *   for us you sweat those drops of blood,*
> *   for us you trod the winepress of divine wrath,*
> *   for us you satisfied the claims of divine justice,*
> *   for us, who were not only unworthy*
> *   but offending creatures,*

whose sins gave you more reasons to hate us
than our misery gave you reasons to pity us.
Though we deserved to die by your power,
you were crucified for us by your love.

This death is the basis of every good thing we enjoy.
Whatever we have is a fruit that grew upon the cross.
Had you not suffered,
we would have been rejected for ever from the throne of God.
Salvation would never have appeared
except through those groans and agonies.
By this alone was God pleased,
and by this our souls find pleasure for ever.
Without it God would have been for ever displeased with us,
and we would have been odious in his sight.

Nothing is such an evidence of your love as your cross;
the miracles you wrought
and the cures you performed during your life
were nothing compared to the kindness of your death.
You were willing to be counted worse
than a murderer in your punishment,
that you might accomplish our deliverance.
The angels in heaven, in their glittering lustre,
are monuments of your generosity,
but not of such supreme affection
as is engraved on the body of your cross.

All love and thankfulness is due to you, Father,
for you gave us your Son,
not only to live but to die for us:
a death so shameful,
a death so accursed,
a death so sharp,
all so that we might repossess the happiness we had lost.

How thankful we are, Father God, for a crucified Redeemer.
Nothing in heaven or earth
    is such an amazing wonder as this;
nothing can compete with it for excellence.

May all the many charms of sin
be overcome by this ravishing love,
which bubbles up in every drop of our Redeemer's blood.
How can we, with thoughts of the cross alive in our hearts,
sin against so much tenderness, compassion and grace,
and all the other perfections of you, our God,
which sound so loud in our ears from the cross of Jesus?
Shall we consider him hanging there to deliver us from hell
    and stain,
and retain any desire to walk in the way
    which led him there?
Can we take any pleasure
    in that which caused so much pain for our best friend?
Can we love that which brought a curse
    better than him who bore the curse for us?
Can we study Christ crucified and still walk on in sin,
    as if he suffered to purchase a license for it
    rather than the destruction of it?
May the consideration of this death
    incline our wills to new desires and resolutions.
May it stifle that luxury, ambition and worldliness
    which harass our souls.
May we not rush into iniquity
    through the wounds of Christ.
Hearing his dying groans,
    may we not cherish that for which he suffered.

Stephen Charnock (1628-1680)[7]

WEDNESDAY

THE LORD OUR LOVER

"The LORD ... will take great delight in you; in his love
he will no longer rebuke you, but will rejoice over
you with singing."
(Zephaniah 3 v 17)

We have a singing God! It's an amazing thought. The infinite love of God is seen most clearly at the cross. That's where we see the vast gulf between our provocations and the price Christ paid to redeem us. But this, says the 18th-century English theologian Anne Dutton, was not the end of Christ's love. Christ not only rescues us from sin; he also embraces us as his bride. He takes delight in us. He rejoices over us. He sings his love to us. A compassionate person might take pity on a hideous creature, but only Christ would take us as his own, embrace us in our ugliness and beautify us through his grace. Can you hear his love song to you? It comes to you today in the gospel message. And it is embodied in bread and wine.

Lord Jesus, we blush with shame,
for though we are the objects of your heart's delight,
*   we wound and pierce you daily by our sins.*
To our shame we count you unworthy of us,
*   though we are poor, base, little selves,*
and yet you gave your great, glorious, matchless Self
*   for us and to us!*

If you, Lord, were to smite us dead, yes, to the lowest hell,
we would deserve it.

Oh, the infinite grace of your heart!
Rather than lose us,
you took our place, our nature, our guilt,
and, yes, our sins as well,
upon your holy, harmless, spotless, glorious Self!
That by your great and righteous Self,
sacrificed for us,
you might purge us from all iniquity,
make us perfect in beauty,
and exalt us in and with you,
to inherit the throne of glory!

Oh, infinite patience, a patience that flows from,
is maintained by,
and resolved into
an infinity of love!
This is ten thousand times more than we deserve!
It is grace that none could show but the God of all grace:
higher than the heaven,
deeper than the sea,
broader than the earth,
longer than time,
long and boundless as eternity!

But, oh, even this is not the end of your love.
For to show your glory and reveal your heart,
you kiss and embrace us!
You rejoice over us with joy and singing (Zephaniah 3 v 17),
as if we were altogether lovely and delightfully fair!
Though you are our God and our Maker, we hear you say:
"You have stolen my heart,
my sister, my bride" (Song of Songs 4 v 9).

"How beautiful you are and how pleasing,
my love, with your delights!" (Song of Songs 7 v 6)
This is your voice to the most vile, ungrateful worms
whom you love and call your bride!
Oh, what dark creatures we are,
and yet you call us fair and your fair ones!
Oh, stupendous grace!
Wonder at it, you blessed angels!
Praise Emmanuel's love, you winged flames!

Oh, that our hearts would melt and break
and be filled with love, under this
all-penetrating,
all-subduing,
all-surpassing love!
Glory to the Lord our Lover!

When we are made perfect in love,
then we at last will love you
with our whole heart, soul, and strength,
without weakness, without weariness:
all love, all duty, all obedience.
We will cast down our crowns
at your royal feet,
at those feet once pierced for us.
We will adore you, the Prince of life,
and shout the praises of your knowledge-surpassing love
throughout the ages without end!

Anne Dutton (1692-1765)[8]

THURSDAY

EAT AND BE SATISFIED

"The poor will eat and be satisfied;
those who seek the LORD will praise him—
may your hearts live for ever!"
(Psalm 22 v 26)

This verse is taken from the psalm that begins "My God, my God, why have you forsaken me?"—the words uttered by Jesus as he hung on the cross under the judgment of God. The first half of the psalm speaks powerfully of the sufferings Jesus would undergo as he died for his people. But the mood changes radically in the second half of the psalm. We move from suffering to triumph. Jesus suffered on the cross, but through his suffering he triumphed over sin and death. Verse 26 is an invitation that flows from the triumph of the cross. Hearts that once were terrified by death are now filled with praise. As the great church father Augustine reminds us, it is a reassurance that is reinforced when we take bread and wine in communion. As we eat, our fears are calmed and our emptiness is satisfied.

How you have loved us, O good Father,
"who did not spare his own Son,
but gave him up for us all" (Romans 8 v 32),
for us wicked ones!
How you have loved us,
for whose sake

Jesus "did not consider equality with [you]
something to be used to his own advantage ...
becoming obedient to death—
even death on a cross!" (Philippians 2 v 6, 8)
He alone was "free among the dead" (Psalm 88 v 5, KJV),
with the power to lay down his life
and the power to take it again (John 10 v 18).
For us he was
both Victor and Victim,
and the Victor because he was the Victim.
For us he was
both the Priest and the Sacrifice,
and the Priest because he was the Sacrifice.
He made slaves into sons,
by being eternally born of you and serving us.

Rightly, then, is my hope strongly fixed on him:
my hope that you will heal all my diseases
through him who sits at your right hand
and makes intercession for us.
Without Jesus I should utterly despair,
for numerous and great are my infirmities,
numerous and great indeed.
But your medicine is greater.

Terrified by my sins and the weight of my misery,
I had racked my heart
and thought of fleeing into the wilderness.
But you strengthened me by saying,
"[Christ] died for all,
that those who live
should no longer live for themselves
but for him who died for them
and was raised again" (2 Corinthians 5 v 15).

Behold, Lord,
I cast my care upon you
that I may live.
> *"Open my eyes that I may see*
> *wonderful things in your law" (Psalm 119 v 18).*
You know my inexperience and my infirmities;
> *teach me and heal me.*
Your only Son—
> *"in whom are hidden all the treasures*
> *of wisdom and knowledge" (Colossians 2 v 3).*
> *has redeemed me with his blood.*
"Remove from me their scorn and contempt"
(Psalm 119 v 22),
as I remember my ransom.
I eat it and drink it and share it in communion.
In my poverty I desire to be satisfied by Christ,
together with all those who eat and are satisfied.
For "the poor will eat and be satisfied;
> *those who seek the LORD will praise him—*
> *may your hearts live for ever!" (Psalm 22 v 26)*

Augustine of Hippo (354-430)[9]

FRIDAY

SURPASSING KNOWLEDGE

"And I pray that you, being rooted and established in love, may have power, together with all the Lord's holy people, to grasp how wide and long and high and deep is the love of Christ, and to know this love that surpasses knowledge—that you may be filled to the measure of all the fullness of God."
(Ephesians 3 v 17-19)

In today's prayer, Charles Spurgeon marshals all his considerable powers of oratory to express the love of Christ. Like Isaac Ambrose (in the reading for Sunday of Week 1), Spurgeon tries to quantify Christ's love by measuring the distance between what he came from and what he came to: "from the height of majesty in glory to the depths of shame on earth". But Spurgeon, like Paul in Ephesians 3, readily admits that describing Christ's love cannot be done. Yet, even though Christ's love is something that "surpasses knowledge", Paul still prays that his readers might "know this love".

We will never bottom out Christ's boundless love. But we need to see more and more of his love. Every time we sin, we need to appreciate afresh this love that welcomes sinners. Every time we suffer, we need to appreciate afresh this love that mysteriously works all things for our good. Every time we face temptation, we need to appreciate afresh this love that captures our hearts.

Your love, O Christ,
in its sweetness,
   its fulness,
      its greatness,
         its faithfulness
surpasses all human comprehension.
Where shall language be found
which shall describe
   your matchless love,
      your unparalleled love,
         towards the children of men?
Your love is so vast and boundless
that, as the swallow skims the water
   without diving into its depths,
so all descriptive words
   merely touch the surface of your love,
   while depths immeasurable lie beneath.
For your love took you
   from the height of majesty in glory
   to the depths of shame on earth.

Who, Lord Jesus, can tell of your majesty?
When you were enthroned in the highest heavens,
you were very God of very God.
By you were the heavens made
and all the hosts within them.
Your own almighty arm upheld the spheres.
The praises of cherubim and seraphim
   perpetually surrounded you.
The full chorus of the hallelujahs of the universe
   unceasingly flowed to the foot of your throne.
You reigned supreme above all your creatures,
God over all, blessed for ever.
Who can tell the height of your glory?

And who can tell how low you descended?
To become a man was something;
to become a man of sorrows was far more;
to bleed, and die, and suffer—
    these were much for you, who were the Son of God.
But to suffer such unparalleled agony—
    to endure a death of shame
    and desertion by your Father—
        this is a depth of condescending love.

The most inspired mind
    must utterly fail to fathom this love.
Here is love!
And truly it is love
    that surpasses knowledge.

Oh, let this love fill our hearts with adoring gratitude
and lead us to practical manifestations of its power.

Charles Spurgeon (1834-1892)[10]

SATURDAY

A CANDLE TO A MIGHTY FLAME

*"I have been crucified with Christ and I no longer live,
but Christ lives in me. The life I now live in the body,
I live by faith in the Son of God, who loved me
and gave himself for me."*
(Galatians 2 v 20)

All my sin and self-confidence have been crucified with Christ ("I have been crucified with Christ"). I no longer depend on my own resources or live for my own glory ("I no longer live"). The poverty of my pride was exposed at the cross. Instead, I now depend on the resources of Christ ("Christ lives in me") giving me new life through the Holy Spirit. So "I live through faith in the Son of God", daily seeking help from him. Love is now the motive and guide of my actions. But how do I keep my love for Christ warm? By reminding myself of his love for us ("who loved me and gave himself for me"). This week we've been considering the love of God revealed in the cross of Christ. Today, Isaac Ambrose invites us to respond. He invites us to address our own soul, calling on our soul to live in Christ and to love Christ.

> *Oh, my soul,*
> *come here and put your little candle to this mighty flame.*
> *If you had ten hearts, all would be too little for Jesus Christ.*
> *Yet go as far as you can,*
> *and love him with the heart you have;*

yes, love him with all your heart,
*   and all your soul, and all your might.*
As Christ in loving you is not his own,
*   so let your soul in loving Christ be not its own:*
*   come, love your Christ, and not yourself;*
*   possess your Christ, and not yourself;*
*   enjoy your Christ, and not yourself;*
*   live in your Christ, and not in yourself;*
*   comfort yourself in your Christ, and not in yourself.*
Say with the apostle,
*   "I have been crucified with Christ*
*   and I no longer live,*
*   but Christ lives in me" (Galatians 2 v 20).*
If you ever come to love Christ truly,
you cannot but deny yourself, and all created rivals.
This love will fix you high above the world,
*   high above your flesh,*
*   high above yourself,*
*   and high above all other loves.*
Nothing in heaven or on earth
will be able to compete with Christ.
Oh, for a soul filled up with all the fulness of God!
Oh, for a soul stretched out to its widest capacity
*   that it might truly enjoy God!*
Oh, for a soul "to grasp
*   how wide and long and high and deep*
*   is the love of Christ, and to know this love*
*   that surpasses knowledge" (Ephesians 3 v 18-19).*
Surely if Christ be mine,
*   if his death be mine,*
*   his resurrection mine,*
*   his ascension mine,*
*   his reign mine,*
*   his intercession mine,*

how should I but love him with a singular love?
Farewell world and worldly glory—
when Christ comes into your room,
it is time for you to vanish.
I shall care little for a candle
when the sun shines fair and bright upon my head.
What, is my name written on the heart of Christ?
Is he at every turn presenting me before his heavenly Father?
Does he wear me as a love-token about his neck?
> *"You have stolen my heart," my King, my Jesus;*
> *"you have stolen my heart with one glance of your eyes,*
> *with one jewel of your necklace" (Song of Songs 4 v 9).*

Suppose, my soul, that you had been there with Christ
when he washed his disciples' feet,
and that he should have washed your feet.
Would not your heart have glowed with love to Jesus Christ?
Why, Christ is now in glory,
and now he takes your filthy soul and dirty duties,
and washes (as it were) the feet of them all
that he may present them to his Father.
You cannot shed a tear
without Jesus washing it over again in his precious blood
and perfuming it with his glorious intercessions.
Oh, what reasons you have to love Jesus Christ!
Oh, you that never loved Christ, come, love him now;
and you that have loved Christ a little, love him more.
Come to be warmed with the love of Christ,
> *and with a love for Christ.*

Isaac Ambrose (1604-1664)[11]

The welcome of Grace

SUNDAY

LOVE BADE ME WELCOME

"Come, all you who are thirsty, come to the waters;
and you who have no money, come, buy and eat!
Come, buy wine and milk
without money and without cost."
(Isaiah 55 v 1)

The cross is an invitation to come home to God. The penalty of sin has been paid at the cross, and so the way to God is open. The prophet Isaiah invites us to a meal. It's a picture of finding true satisfaction in God. There is no cost to us because the price has been paid by Christ. Today we have two poems by George Herbert, the 17th-century Welsh poet and clergyman. The first poem, "The Agony", reminds us that if we want to see the enormity of human sin, then we should look at the cross. But it also reminds us that the cross reveals the enormity of divine love. For God-in-Christ, love meant shedding his blood (the word "abroach" in the third verse means "to pierce in order to release liquid"). And so for us, God's love now means drinking wine. It's a picture of the eternal banquet in God's presence promised by Isaiah, but it's also a promise we anticipate every time we take communion. In the second poem Herbert hesitates to come to this feast, but God (personified in the poem as Love) gently persuades him. (To make the "conversation" between God and the sinner clearer I've added quotation marks.)

The Agony

Philosophers have measur'd mountains,
fathom'd the depths of the seas, of states, and kings,
walk'd with a staff to heav'n, and traced fountains:
but there are two vast, spacious things,
the which to measure it doth more behove:
yet few there are that sound them: Sin and Love.

Who would know Sin, let him repair
unto mount Olivet; there shall he see
a man so wrung with pains, that all his hair,
his skin, his garments bloody be.
Sin is that press and vice, which forceth pain
to hunt his cruel food through ev'ry vein.

Who knows not Love, let him assay
and taste that juice, which on the cross a pike
did set again abroach, then let him say
if ever he did taste the like.
Love is that liquor sweet and most divine,
which my God feels as blood; but I, as wine.

Love

Love bade me welcome. Yet my soul drew back,
    guilty of dust and sin.
But quick-eyed Love, observing me grow slack
    from my first entrance in,
drew nearer to me, sweetly questioning,
    If I lacked any thing.

"A guest," I answered, "worthy to be here".
    Love said, "You shall be he".
"I, the unkind, ungrateful? Ah my dear,
    I cannot look on thee."

Love took my hand, and smiling did reply,
  "Who made the eyes, but I?"

"Truth Lord, but I have marred them: let my shame
  go where it doth deserve."
"And know you not," says Love, "who bore the blame?"
  "My dear, then I will serve."
"You must sit down," says Love, "and taste my meat".
  So I did sit and eat.

George Herbert (1593-1633)[12]

MONDAY

A BETTER WORD

"We have an advocate with the Father—Jesus Christ, the Righteous One. He is the atoning sacrifice for our sins."
(1 John 2 v 1-2)

What do we see as we come in faith before the throne of God? We see Jesus our advocate. It's legal language. Jesus is our defence lawyer, pleading our case before the Judge. And what is that case? Jesus himself. He is "the atoning sacrifice for our sins". It's a term that describes turning aside wrath. God's anger at our sin was absorbed in full by Jesus at the cross. This doesn't mean the Father was, or is, in any way reluctant to welcome us. God himself sent Jesus to be our atoning sacrifice, and God himself appointed Jesus to be our advocate. As the 19th-century Scottish preacher and theologian William Symington reminds us, Christ intercedes for us to illuminate God's grace and reassure our hearts.

Gracious Father, we come to you in faith
because in the midst of the throne stands Jesus,
a Lamb "looking as if it had been slain" (Revelation 5 v 6).
The robes of our exalted Mediator
*   do not conceal the marks of our Mediator's suffering;*
the diadem of glory
*   does not hide the impression left by the crown of thorns.*
He is still red in his apparel,
and his garments dyed with blood.

The scars of conflict are visible in the body of the Conqueror.
His wounds are still open,
 and every mouth pleads our cause before you.
His death pleads for our life;
 his blood cries for our safety;
  his tears procure our comfort;
   and everlasting joy is borne to us
    on the breeze of his deep-drawn sighs.

Thus the sacrifice of our Redeemer—
the wounds in his hands and his feet,
 and his transfixed side,
plead the cause of his people
 with perfect clarity,
  and infallible power.
The Advocate and the Atonement are the same:
"We have an advocate with the Father …
He is the atoning sacrifice for our sins" (1 John 2 v 1-2).
The prayers of Christ breathe the sweetness,
and produce the effects, of incense.

It is not because it is necessary to express his will
 that Christ appears before you.
Christ does not intercede on our behalf
to remind you
 of what you would otherwise forget,
or to make known to you
 what you would otherwise not know,
or to incline you
 to that which you would otherwise not choose.
No, it is to illustrate and illuminate
 the divine majesty and holiness;
to display the wisdom, grace, and merits of the Son;
to impress on us, his redeemed people,
 our obligations to deep and lasting gratitude.

And one thing is certain,
that such is the effectiveness of the Saviour's blood,
    such is the value of his death,
       such is the merit of his sacrifice,
that the reminders of his atonement,
    exhibited before you, the God of heaven,
advocate our cause more powerfully
    than could ever be done through human language.
No tongue of an orator or eloquence of an angel
can ever plead so effectually in favour of guilty sinners
    as "the sprinkled blood
    that speaks a better word
    than the blood of Abel" (Hebrews 12 v 24).

William Symington (1795-1862)[13]

TUESDAY

SUCH A SOUL-FRIEND

"The Son of Man came eating and drinking,
and you say, 'Here is a glutton and a drunkard,
a friend of tax collectors and sinners.'"
(Luke 7 v 34)

In this verse Jesus is repeating the accusation of the religious leaders. As far as they are concerned it is an insult to be called a friend of sinners. It carries the taint of guilt by association. But Jesus glories in this title. Indeed the next thing that happens in Luke's Gospel is that Jesus welcomes a notoriously sinful woman. So much for guilt by association—Jesus embraces it! Ultimately, Jesus took our guilt entirely on himself as he died in our place at the cross: "God made him who had no sin to be sin for us, so that in him we might become the righteousness of God" (2 Corinthians 5 v 21). Here is the true friend of sinners, and his cross is the ultimate act of friendship! Today the Puritan James Janeway pleads with us to make Jesus our friend. Every way you look at Jesus, he makes a great friend!

If kindness and love are what you seek,
*   there is no one as sweet or generous as Jesus.*
If comfort and pleasure are what you desire,
*   there is no one, when the soul is surrounded*
*   with a multitude of perplexities,*
*   who can so much delight, refresh and raise it.*

If power and majesty,
with the ability to defend from injuries and revenge wrongs,
signify anything to poor fragile creatures,
    there is no one yet who has ever overcome Jesus.
    For who ever contended with God and prospered?
If vigour and care in all our affairs
can entice the helpless sinner,
    there is no one who will take more care of us
    and do more for us than Jesus.
If freedom of access,
despite the infinite distance between us,
signify anything that might commend a friend,
    there is no better welcome for a poor beggar
    than at the house of this mighty Prince.
If faithfulness in the greatest difficulties
raise the esteem of a friend,
    no one has ever trusted Jesus and been let down.
Are riches and wealth worth having?
    There is no one who can give a kingdom
    as a token of love,
    and give everlasting glory and heaven, except Jesus.
Do pity in misery,
    sympathy in suffering,
        compassion in distress
            endear and commend a friend?
    There is no one more tender-hearted than Jesus.
Are honours and promotions such great things?
    Jesus will make his chosen people kings and priests,
    setting them on thrones,
    and commending them before the whole world.
Is suitability a consideration to make this match?
    There is no one better suited to satisfy our desires
    than the infinite One.

Do poor simple creatures,
who have undone themselves by their folly and indiscretion,
need a wise counsellor to untangle their sad intricacies?
    There is no one among the profound politicians
    and grave sages of the world
    to be compared to Jesus.
Does a dying man with a never-dying soul,
that is to pass into an eternal state,
lack a never-dying and immortal Friend?
    There is no one else who can stand by him
    for God alone is immortal.
Are not friends sometimes furthest away
when one has most need of them?
    Then Jesus is a Friend to be highly prized,
    since he will never be absent,
    for does not God fill heaven and earth?
What do you think of such a Soul-friend?
Is not such a one worth seeking:
one who will ensure your soul reaches its destination?
    There is no one who ever did more for souls than Christ.
Would it not be true prudence
    to make sure of such a Friend—
a Friend we must have for our Friend,
or else we will be miserable for ever?

James Janeway (1636-1674)[14]

WEDNESDAY

STARS DWELLING WITH DUST

*"Once you were alienated from God and were enemies in
your minds because of your evil behaviour. But now he has
reconciled you by Christ's physical body through death to
present you holy in his sight, without blemish
and free from accusation."*
(Colossians 1 v 21-22)

Sin is a declaration of war. It is an act of revolution in
which we depose our rightful King and try to put ourselves in his place. So ever since the Garden of Eden, human
beings have been enemies of God. Until Jesus. Jesus came to
bring peace. Jesus died a rebel's death to reconcile rebels to
God. The wide gulf between us and God has been bridged
at the cross. And so now God offers a peace treaty. Today
James Janeway continues his exhortation to come to God
through Jesus and then gives us words of praise to respond
to God's gracious invitation. Humanity was made from the
dust of the earth (Genesis 2 v 7). But in his love God has
condescended to embrace the dust, make a covenant with
the dust and dwell with the dust. How can we refuse?

> *What do you say now?*
> *Are you resolved to come to Jesus or not?*
> *Shall the infinite Majesty of heaven condescend*
>   *to offer himself to be loved*
>   *and embraced by sinful dust,*

and shall God say,
  "I will be your Father!"
and shall not the sinner say,
  "I would be your child!"?
Why should the heart
of every apostate and rebellious traitor
who has forfeited life and soul
not leap at such good news and say,
    "Will God, despite everything, lay aside the conflict
    and conclude a peace?
    Will he receive rebels with mercy?
    Will he open his doors to prodigals?
    Is there still the possibility of hope?
    Is it possible that such sins as mine
        should be forgiven?
    Can it be conceived that a creature like me
        should be embraced?
    What! Look upon me!
        Will God indeed take me into his favour?"
            Yes, you!
Behold he calls you,
he offers you his Son,
  a kingdom,
    a crown.
Look, the Father meets us.
Look, he hastens to greet his returning prodigal (Luke 15 v 20).

And now, Lord God,
what shall your servants say to you?
For we are silenced with wonder
and must sit down with astonishment
for we cannot utter the least jot of your praises.
What does the height of this strange love mean?
Oh, that the God of heaven and earth

should condescend to enter into
* a covenant with his dust,*
and to take to his heart
* the viperous brood that have spat their venom in his face!*
We are not worthy
* to be your servants.*
How much less are we worthy
* to be your children and heirs,*
* and to become partakers*
* of all those blessed liberties and privileges*
* which you have settled upon us!*
But for your goodness' sake
and according to your own heart,
you have done all these great things.

We are astonished and ravished with wonder.
For the infinite breach is made up;
* the offender is received;*
*   God and man are reconciled.*
A covenant of peace has been made;
* heaven and earth have agreed on the terms;*
*   they have shaken hands and signed the contract!*
Happy conclusion!
Blessed conjunction!
Shall the stars dwell with the dust?
Shall the wide-distant poles,
* north and south, east and west, embrace together?*
But here an infinitely greater distance has been bridged.

James Janeway (1636-1674)[15]

THURSDAY

A BOTTOMLESS OCEAN OF GRACE

*"Surely God is my salvation; I will trust and not be afraid.
The LORD, the LORD himself, is my strength and my defence;
he has become my salvation. With joy you will draw water
from the wells of salvation."*
(Isaiah 12 v 2-3)

Who is our Saviour? The prophet Isaiah is in no doubt: "God is my salvation". Indeed, he is emphatic: "The LORD, the LORD himself ... has become my salvation". Only God is strong enough to save. But what about the problem of judgment? Who will pay the penalty of our sin? It is a penalty that humanity should pay but cannot; and it is a penalty God can pay but should not. The answer is the God-man. The result is a bottomless ocean of grace from which we may draw for ever. As the Puritan John Owen puts it, the conduit of Christ's humanity is inseparably united to the inexhaustible fountain of his deity. In other words, Christ's humanity is the pipe that connects us to an unending supply of divine grace. It is a well of salvation which will never run dry.

Lord Jesus Christ,
we praise you for the endless, bottomless, boundless
grace and compassion we find in you:
you, who are both our husband and the God of Zion.

The grace of a creature will not serve our needs—
we are too impoverished for such a supply.
There was a fullness of grace in your human nature
for God gave you "the Spirit without limit" (John 3 v 34).
It is a fullness like light in the sun and water in the sea:
a fullness incomparably above the measure of angels.
Yet it was not truly an infinite fullness
for it was created and therefore limited.
If it could be conceived separately from your deity,
then surely so many thirsty, guilty souls,
as every day drink deep and large draughts of grace,
would (if I may so speak) sink you to the very bottom.

But the conduit of your humanity is inseparably united to
the infinite:
    the inexhaustible
        fountain of the Deity.
And who can look into its depths?
There is grace enough for sinners
    in an all-sufficient God,
        and it is found in you, Lord Jesus.
We hear your word,
bringing peace and confidence to sinners:
    "Do not be afraid; you will not be put to shame.
    Do not fear disgrace;
    you will not be humiliated" (Isaiah 54 v 4).
But how shall this be?
So much sin and not ashamed?
So much guilt and not confounded?
    "For your Maker is your husband—
        the LORD Almighty is his name—
    the Holy One of Israel is your Redeemer;
        he is called the God of all the earth" (Isaiah 54 v 5).
This is the bottom of all peace,

all confidence, all consolation:
the grace and mercy
of you, our Maker,
of you, the God of the whole earth.

If all the world should set themselves
to drink free grace, mercy, and pardon,
drawing water continually from the wells of salvation—
if they should set themselves to draw water
with an angel standing by, and crying,
"Drink, O my friends, yes, drink abundantly;
take as much grace and pardon
as shall be abundantly sufficient for the world of sin
which is in every one of you"—
they would not be able to sink the grace of the promise
one hair's breadth.
There is enough for millions of worlds,
because it flows from an infinite, bottomless fountain.
"Do not be afraid, you worm Jacob" (Isaiah 41 v 14),
"for I am God, and not a man" (Hosea 11 v 9).
This is the ground of a sinner's consolation,
the most precious fountain of grace and mercy.
This infinite grace answers all objections
that might hinder our souls
from drawing near to communion with you
and from freely embracing you.
Will not this match our needs in all our distresses?
What is our finite guilt before infinite grace?
There is no sinner who can spread his iniquities
to the dimensions of this grace?
Here is mercy enough for the greatest, the oldest,
the most stubborn transgressor.
We will not let anyone rob us of our confidence in your deity.

John Owen (1616-1683)[16]

FRIDAY

A HIGHWAY TO HIS HEART

*"He is able to deal gently with those who are
ignorant and are going astray, since he himself is
subject to weakness."*
(Hebrews 5 v 2)

Without Christ, God is a source of terror because of his relentless opposition to sin. It is only through Christ that we can come before a holy God. But this doesn't mean God the Father is reluctant to save and has to be won over by the Son. Yes, we need a mediator, but it is God himself who appoints Jesus as our mediator: "Christ did not take on himself the glory of becoming a high priest ... [but he] was designated by God to be high priest" (Hebrews 5 v 5, 10). In his love, God has found a way to welcome sinners while remaining true to his justice, and that way is Jesus. So what kind of a mediator is Jesus? One who knows exactly what it's like for us to struggle and suffer. He never looks on us with disdain, saying, *What's all the fuss about?* Think about the temptations or trials you face today. Jesus looks on you in those struggles with compassion. So today Charles Spurgeon exhorts us to come to Christ. Hear his words as an invitation from Christ to your soul, and then use the words he suggests to come to Christ.

*Sinner, you are not asked to draw near to the consuming Fire.
You might well tremble to approach the God*

whom you have so grievously offended.
But there is a man ordained
 to mediate between you and God,
and if you would come to God,
 you must come through him—the man Christ Jesus.
God apart from Christ is a source of terror
 for he will by no means spare the guilty.
But look at the Son of Man!
He is a man with hands full of blessing,
 eyes wet with tears of pity,
  lips overflowing with love
   and a heart melting with tenderness.
Do you not see the gash in his side?
Through that wound there is a highway to his heart,
and anyone who needs his compassion may access it.
Oh, sinners! The way to the Saviour's heart is open,
 and penitent seekers shall never be denied.
Why should even the most despairing
 be afraid to approach the Saviour?
If you are weak,
 your weakness will touch his sympathy,
and your sad inability
 will be an argument with his abounding mercy.
Sinner, place yourself by an act of faith today
 beneath the cross of Jesus;
 look up to him and say,
 "Blessed Physician,
 whose wounds for me can heal me,
 whose death for me can make me live,
 look down upon me!
You are human: you know what human beings suffer.
You are human: will you let a human being
 sink down to hell who cries to you for help?
You are human, and you can save:

will you let a poor unworthy one who longs for mercy
be driven into hopeless misery,
while they cry to you to let your merits save them?"

Oh, guilty ones,
have faith that you can reach the heart of Jesus.
Sinner, fly to Jesus without fear; he waits to save.
It is his role to receive sinners and reconcile them to God.
May the Holy Spirit lead you to devout meditation
upon the humility of our Lord; and so may you find
the door of life,
the portal of peace,
the gate of heaven!

Every child of God ought to be comforted
by the fact that our Redeemer is one of our own race.
How completely it takes the bitterness out of grief
to know that it once was suffered by him.
This day we can bear
poverty, slander, contempt, bodily pain and death itself
because Jesus Christ our Lord has borne it.
By his humiliation
it shall become a pleasure to be abased for his sake.
By the spittle that distilled down his cheeks
it shall become a fair thing to be made a mockery for him.
By the buffeting and the blindfolding
it shall become an honour to be disgraced.
By the cross it shall become life itself
to surrender life for so precious a Master!
May the Man of sorrows now appear to us
and enable us to bear our sorrows cheerfully.
If there is consolation anywhere, surely it is to be found
in the delightful presence of the Crucified.

Charles Spurgeon (1834-1892)[17]

SATURDAY

PERFUMED BY JESUS

*"Through Jesus, therefore, let us continually offer to God a
sacrifice of praise—the fruit of lips that openly profess his
name. And do not forget to do good and to share with others,
for with such sacrifices God is pleased."*
(Hebrews 13 v 15-16)

The writer of Hebrews has repeatedly stressed that the sacrifice of Jesus is a "once for all" sacrifice that has completely dealt with sin (Hebrews 7 v 26-27; 9 v 25-28; 10 v 10-14). So we cannot, and need not, make sacrifices to win God's approval because Christ provides complete salvation. And yet it is our privilege to be priests offering sacrifices to God. We do not offer a sacrifice to deal with sin—Christ has already done that. We offer "a sacrifice of praise"—lips and lives that honour God. But if we're honest, we know that even our service of God is tainted by sin and pride. So how can our service of God be acceptable to God? The answer lies in the opening words of verse 15: "through Jesus". Here's how William Symington puts it: "Far from the performances of men being the ground of their acceptance with God, it thus appears that for the acceptance of our performances themselves we are indebted to the merits of another [that is, Jesus]".

Gracious Father,
we come before you in the name of Jesus Christ.
He made peace by the blood of his cross;

this peace is maintained
as he presents his blood in heaven.
He reconciled us to you by his death;
we remain reconciled through his life of intercession.
There are many things which disturb this peace
and break this state of reconciliation.
Sin separates us from you, our God;
the accusations of Satan and a guilty conscience
deprive us of inward tranquillity.
But, through the Saviour's intercession,
may the propitiation for sin be so applied,
and his sprinkled blood so brought home to the conscience,
that any interruption of communion or peace
becomes only partial and temporary.
"'Though the mountains be shaken
and the hills be removed,
yet my unfailing love for you will not be shaken
nor my covenant of peace be removed,' says the LORD,
who has compassion on you" (Isaiah 54 v 10).
We, your people, always have access to you
for the supply of our daily needs.
Not a day, not an hour, goes by
without us having business in the court of heaven:
requests to make;
sins to be pardoned;
needs to be supplied;
iniquities to confess with shame;
blessings to acknowledge with gratitude.
And how shall we approach a throne of such awful majesty?
How shall we enter a court of such inexorable justice?
The Mediator before the throne,
the Advocate at the bar, is our encouragement.
"Through him we … have access
to the Father by one Spirit" (Ephesians 2 v 18).

*"In him and through faith in him we may approach God
with freedom and confidence" (Ephesians 3 v 12).*

*It is through the intercession of Christ
that our service is rendered acceptable.
The law requires perfection,
but we confess that our best services are imperfect.
The law requires unblemished obedience,
but we confess our best services are tainted with pollution.
How then shall they be accepted?
Through the intercession of your Son.
This makes up for all our deficiencies;
this removes all our blemishes.
And what is true of our prayers
is also true of all our other services—
 our songs of praise,
  our tears of penitence,
   our works of faith,
    our labours of love,
     our deeds of mercy
      and our acts of holy obedience.
 "Their burnt offerings and sacrifices
 will be accepted on my altar" (Isaiah 56 v 7).*

*Through Jesus may you overlook all our imperfections;
may our actions become a sweet aroma;
may our sacrifices become acceptable in your sight.
Though our sacrifices rise like "a column of smoke",
 confused and ill-savoured,
they come before you
 "perfumed with myrrh and incense made from
  all the spices of the merchant" (Song of Songs 3 v 6).*

William Symington (1795-1862)[18]

The Exchange of Places

SUNDAY

THE STARS WERE CONFOUNDED

"For Christ also suffered once for sins, the righteous for the
unrighteous, to bring you to God."
(1 Peter 3 v 18)

At the cross an amazing exchange took place. Jesus took on himself both the shame and the penalty of our sin. What makes this all the more extraordinary is that as almighty God what he actually deserved was not shame, but honour; and as the perfectly holy One what he actually deserved was not judgment but vindication. As a result of this amazing exchange, another amazing exchange takes place for his people. Instead of the shame that we ought to have as a result of our sinful nature, we receive glory as a result of God's gracious love. Instead of the condemnation we deserve, we are declared righteous (in the right before God). A swap has taken place: Jesus takes our judgment and gives us his reward. The 3rd-century church father Cyprian reminds us that we see this great exchange in every aspect of the story of Christ's passion.

Precious Saviour,
even before your Passion reached the cruelty of death
and the shedding of blood,
what infamies of reproach you patiently heard,
what mockings of contempt you suffered.
You had used your spit to heal a blind man;

yet for us you received the spittings of insulters!
In your name the devil and his angels are beaten;
    yet for us you suffered beatings!
You crown martyrs with eternal flowers;
    yet for us you were crowned with thorns.
You give victory palm branches to those who overcome;
    yet for us you were struck on the face with palms.
You clothe us with immortality;
    yet for us you were stripped of your earthly garments.
You give us heavenly food;
    yet for us you were fed with bitter gall.
You hold the cup of salvation;
    yet for us you were given vinegar to drink.
You are guiltless, the just One;
indeed, you are innocence itself and justice itself,
    yet for us you were counted among transgressors
    and truth was suppressed with false witnesses.
You shall judge;
    yet for us you were judged.
You are the Word of God;
    yet for us you were led silently to the slaughter.
When you hung on the cross,
    the stars were confounded,
        the elements were disturbed,
            the earth quaked,
                night shut out the day,
                    the sun withdrew his rays
                    that he might not be compelled
                    to look upon the crime.
You did not speak, nor did you resist,
    nor did you declare your majesty.
To the very end you bore all things with perseverance
that in you a full and perfect patience
    might be consummated.

And after all these things,
you still receive your murderers
if they will turn and come to you;
and with a saving patience
you close your church to no one.
Those adversaries,
   those blasphemers,
      those who were enemies of your name,
if they repent of their sin
and acknowledge their crime—
you receive them,
not only pardoning their sin
but rewarding them with the heavenly kingdom.
Who can be said to be more patient, more merciful?
Even those who shed your blood
   are made alive by that blood—so great is your patience.

   "Christ suffered for you, leaving you an example,
   that you should follow in his steps.
   'He committed no sin,*
   and no deceit was found in his mouth.'
   When they hurled their insults at him, he did not
   retaliate;
   when he suffered, he made no threats.
   Instead, he entrusted himself
   to him who judges justly" (1 Peter 2 v 21-23).

Empower us, who have placed ourselves in you by faith,
who have clothed ourselves with you,
who are on you, the way of salvation;
empower us that we may follow your example.

Cyprian (c. 200-258)[19]

MONDAY

A HAPPY EXCHANGE

*"Grace and peace to you from God our Father
and the Lord Jesus Christ, who gave himself for our sins to
rescue us from the present evil age,
according to the will of our God and Father,
to whom be glory for ever and ever. Amen."
(Galatians 1 v 3-5)*

Jesus is our example. He is the epitome of love and holiness, embodying the attitudes and behaviours that please God. But he is so much more than an example. First and foremost he is our Saviour. Jesus our example is not good news because it is an example we can never live up to. But Jesus our Saviour is the best news ever. Here's how Martin Luther puts it: "We do not deny that the faithful ought to follow the example of Christ. But we say that they are not justified in this way before God. To be made righteous we must set nothing before our eyes but Jesus Christ dying for our sins and rising again for our righteousness. We must see him by faith as a gift and not as an example."

> *What has Christ given?*
> *Not gold, nor silver, nor beasts,*
> *nor Passover lambs, nor an angel*
> *but "himself"!*
> *For what?*
> *Not for a crown, not for a kingdom,*

not for our holiness and righteousness,
but "for our sins"!

Eternal Father,
these words are thunderclaps from heaven
against every kind of self-righteousness.
But they are full consolation,
comforting fearful consciences exceedingly.

For we cannot put away our sins by our own works.
Our sins are so great,
   so infinite,
     so invincible;
it is impossible for the whole world to satisfy for one of them.
The greatness of the ransom—Jesus Christ your Son—
is evidence enough that we can neither satisfy for sin
nor have dominion over it.
Yet Christ has taken upon himself our sins,
bearing your wrath,
not for his own sake, which was just and invincible,
but for our sakes.
Making a happy exchange with us,
he took upon himself our sin
and gave us his innocence and victory,
in which we, being now clothed,
are freed from the curse of the law.
Bearing the sin of the whole world in himself,
he was taken, he suffered, he was crucified and put to death,
becoming a curse for us.
But, because he was a divine and everlasting person,
it was impossible that death should hold him.
Therefore he rose again on the third day and lives for ever.
Neither sin nor death is found in him anymore,
but pure righteousness and life everlasting.

Eternal Father,
may we have this image continually before us
and look at it with the steadfast eye of faith
so that we may share the innocence and victory of Christ,
even though we are ever so great sinners.
Believing that sin, death and the curse
are abolished in Christ,
may they be abolished in us.
Just as there is now no sin or death in Christ,
so may we believe that there is now none in us.
The victory of Christ is certain and without defect;
the problem is our unbelief.
For human reason finds it hard to believe
all these good things and unspeakable riches.
So when sin vexes us and death terrifies us,
help us to regard them as an imagination,
    a false delusion from the devil.

Eternal Father,
all kinds of evil would have overwhelmed us,
as they will overwhelm the wicked for ever.
But Christ, being made for us a transgressor of all laws,
    guilty of all our criminality,
comes between as a mediator,
embracing us wicked and damnable sinners.
He took upon himself all our evils,
which should have oppressed and tormented us for ever.
They cast him down, engulfing his head like water:
    "Your wrath has swept over me;
        your terrors have destroyed me" (Psalm 88 v 16).
So Christ has delivered us from everlasting terrors,
and we shall enjoy an everlasting peace.
This we believe; help us to believe it more.

Martin Luther (1483-1546)[20]

TUESDAY

CHRIST COMES TO YOU IN THE WORD

*"Before your very eyes Jesus Christ was
clearly portrayed as crucified."*
(Galatians 3 v 1)

When did the Galatian Christians see Jesus crucified before their very eyes? After all, they weren't there on that first Good Friday. The answer is that they "saw" Jesus crucified when they "heard" the gospel preached. As John Bunyan, the author of *The Pilgrim's Progress*, puts it, Christ is "set forth in the word of the gospel". And what do we see in the gospel? We see a great exchange: Christ suffers what he does not deserve that we might be set free from the judgment we do deserve. And this is not just theory; this is personal. In the message of Christ we encounter Christ himself. "He comes to you," says Bunyan to the sinner, "in the word of the gospel".

*Here is love, that God sent his Son, his darling,
   his Son that never offended,
   his Son that was always his delight!
Here is love, that God sent him to save sinners,
   to save them by bearing their sins,
     by bearing their curse,
      by dying their death,
       and by carrying their sorrows!*

Here is love:
"When we were still powerless,
Christ died for the ungodly."
"While we were still sinners,
Christ died for us."
"While we were God's enemies,
we were reconciled to him
through the death of his Son" (Romans 5 v 6, 8, 10).

Oh, sinful soul,
the great Bringer of the gospel is the Lord Jesus himself.
He was, and is, set forth in the word of the gospel.
See him making peace with God for you by his blood.
See in the features of his sufferings
every offer of the gospel of his grace to you.
Christ is set forth as betrayed
to save the soul from being betrayed by the devil and sin.
Christ is set forth as apprehended
to save the soul from being apprehended by justice.
Christ is set forth as condemned
to save the soul from being condemned by the law.
Christ is set forth as spat on,
to save the soul from being held in contempt
by the demands of holiness.
Christ is set forth as scourged
to save the soul from being scourged
with the guilt of sins, as with scorpions.
Christ is set forth as buffeted
to save the soul from being continually buffeted
by its own conscience.
Christ is set forth as crowned with thorns
to save the soul from being crowned
with dishonour and shame for ever.
Christ is set forth as crucified

to save the soul from dying the second death.
Christ is set forth as pierced with nails and a spear
to save the soul from wounds and grief for ever.

Do you understand me, sinful soul?
He wrestled with justice
that you might have rest.
He wept and mourned
that you might laugh and rejoice.
He was betrayed
that you might go free.
He was apprehended
that you might escape.
He was condemned
that you might be justified.
He was killed
that you might live.
He wore a crown of thorns
that you might wear a crown of glory.
He was nailed to the cross with his arms wide open
to show with what freeness all his merits
shall be bestowed on the soul that comes to him,
and how warmly he will receive it into his heart?
All these benefits he offers to you freely.
Yes, he comes to you in the word of the gospel,
with the blood running down from his head upon his face,
with his tears remaining on his cheeks,
with the holes still fresh in his hands and his feet,
with the blood still flowing from his side,
to ask you to accept these benefits
and so to be reconciled to God.

John Bunyan (1628-1688)[21]

WEDNESDAY

TODAY WE HAVE CLEAN ESCAPED

"When the LORD goes through the land to strike down the Egyptians, he will see the blood on the top and sides of the door-frame and will pass over that doorway, and he will not permit the destroyer to enter your houses and strike you down."
(Exodus 12 v 23)

Many centuries before Jesus, God had rescued his people from slavery in Egypt through the "exodus". God sent a series of plagues on Egypt which culminated in the death of every firstborn child. God's people escaped this act of judgment by daubing the blood of a sacrificial lamb around their doorposts. The "destroyer" "passed over" every house protected by the blood—an event commemorated in the Passover Festival. Everywhere else in Egypt the judgment of death fell on each household, and the Pharaoh was forced to let God's people go free. This first exodus was designed to illustrate and illuminate the work of Jesus. Jesus is the Passover Lamb, whose blood is "daubed" over our lives. And so through Jesus we experience our own exodus from the slavery of sin and the judgment of death. The church father Gregory of Nazianzus places us in the middle of this story. He retells the exodus as our story and describes what Christ has done as if it were only yesterday.

Eternal Lord,
yesterday the Lamb was slain,
*   the door-posts were anointed,*
*   Egypt bewailed her firstborn,*
*   the Destroyer passed us over,*
while we were walled in with the precious blood.
Today we have clean escaped
from Egypt and from Pharaoh;
and there is no one to hinder us
from keeping the feast: the feast of our departure.
*   "Therefore let us keep the Festival,*
*   not with the old bread leavened*
*   with malice and wickedness,*
*   but with the unleavened bread*
*   of sincerity and truth" (1 Corinthians 5 v 8).*
Yesterday we were crucified with Christ;
*   today we are glorified with him.*
Yesterday we died with him;
*   today we are alive with him.*
Yesterday we were buried with him;
*   today we rise with him.*

Eternal Lord,
we offer to Christ,
who suffered and rose again for us,
not mere gold, or silver, or costly stones;
*   we offer ourselves,*
*   the possession most precious to him*
*   and most fitting for him.*
We give back to the Image
*   what is made after the Image.*
We recognise him as our Dignity;
*   We honour him as our Archetype;*
*   We want to know the power of the mystery.*

Let us become like Christ,
*   since Christ became like us.*
Let us become yours for his sake,
*   since he became man for our sake.*
He assumed the worse
*   that he might give us the best.*
He became poor
*   that we through his poverty might be rich.*
He took upon himself the form of a servant
*   that we might receive back our liberty.*
He came down
*   that we might be exalted.*
He was tempted
*   that we might conquer.*
He was dishonoured
*   that he might glorify us.*
He died
*   that he might save us;*
He ascended
*   that he might draw us to himself,*
*   who had been brought low by our fall into sin.*
Help us, we pray, to give all to him,
*   offer all to him,*
*   who for us gave himself*
*   as a ransom and a reconciliation.*

Gregory of Nazianzus (329-390)[22]

THURSDAY

FURY IS MADE GENTLE

"Where, O death, is your victory?
Where, O death, is your sting?"
(1 Corinthians 15 v 55)

At the cross Christ exchanged places with us: he was condemned to absolve us (declare us free from guilt), and he died to give us life. As a result, a grand exchange has taken place in our lives. Our future has utterly transformed. Christ has turned on their head our current empty way of life and our future condemnation. Where once we lived in fear of death, now through Christ we can taunt it! "Where, O death," we cry, "is your victory?" The 16th-century Reformer John Calvin beautifully captures the complete nature of this transformation.

> *Christ is Isaac, the beloved Son of the Father,*
> *who was offered as a sacrifice*
> *but did not succumb to the power of death.*
> *Christ is Jacob, the watchful shepherd,*
> *who has such great care for the sheep which he guards.*
> *Christ is the compassionate brother Joseph, who in his glory*
> *was not ashamed to acknowledge his brothers,*
> *however lowly and abject their condition.*
> *Christ is the great sacrificer and bishop Melchizedek,*
> *who has offered an eternal sacrifice once for all.*
> *Christ is the sovereign lawgiver Moses,*

writing his law on the tablets of our hearts by his Spirit.
Christ is the faithful captain and guide Joshua,
    leading us to the promised land.
Christ is the victorious and noble King David,
    bringing all rebellious powers to subjection.
Christ is the magnificent and triumphant King Solomon,
    governing his kingdom in peace and prosperity.
Christ is the strong and powerful Samson,
    who by his death has overwhelmed all his enemies.

Every good thing we could conceive or desire
is to be found in Jesus Christ alone.
For he was sold to buy us back;
    captive to deliver us;
        condemned to absolve us;
            cursed for our blessing;
                made a sin offering for our righteousness;
                marred that we may be made fair;
                died for our life.

And so by Christ
    fury is made gentle,
    wrath appeased,
    darkness turned into light,
    fear reassured,
    despisal despised,
    debt cancelled,
    labour lightened,
    sadness made merry,
    misfortune made fortunate,
    difficulty made easy,
    disorder ordered,
    division united,
    ignominy ennobled,
    rebellion subjected,

intimidation intimidated,
ambush uncovered,
assaults assailed,
force forced back,
combat combatted,
war warred against,
vengeance avenged,
torment tormented,
damnation damned,
the abyss sunk into the abyss,
hell transfixed,
death made dead,
mortality made immortal.
In short, mercy has swallowed up all misery,
and goodness has swallowed all misfortune.

All these things which were
the weapons of the devil in his battle against us
are turned to our profit.
By the Spirit of Christ we are seated
among those who are in heaven,
so that for us this world is no more.
For we are content in all things,
whatever our country, status, condition, clothing or food.
We are comforted in tribulation,
joyful in sorrow,
glorying when abused,
abounding in poverty,
warmed in our nakedness,
patient among evils,
living in death.

John Calvin (1509-1564)[23]

FRIDAY

THE MATCHLESS MAN

*"For this reason he had to be made like them, fully human
in every way, in order that he might become a merciful and
faithful high priest in service to God, and that he might
make atonement for the sins of the people."*
(Hebrews 2 v 17)

At Christmas, God became man. The Son became human, truly human, as human as you and I. But even on that first Christmas Day, Easter was in view. Hebrews 2 v 17 gives two reason why Jesus became human. First, Jesus had to experience what it is to be human so he could be a faithful high priest, sympathising with us in our weakness. Second, Jesus had to become human so he could make atonement for our sins. Humanity had sinned so humanity had to pay the penalty for sin. But none of us could pay it. Only God had resources to pay; only humanity had the duty to pay. Step forward the God-Man! Charles Spurgeon describes the humanity of Christ as a "gospel church-bell which must be rung every Sunday". "This is one of those provisions of the Lord's household, which, like bread and salt, should be put upon the table at every spiritual meal."

Lord Jesus Christ,
you were beloved and adored by angels;
*   and you were despised and rejected of men.*
You were worshipped by cherubim and seraphim.

and from you men hid their faces in contempt.
You are God and were with God in the beginning,
*   and you were made flesh and dwelt among us.*
This is the great mystery of godliness:
*   God was manifest in the flesh.*
You who asked the Samaritan woman for a drink,
*   dug the channels of the ocean*
*   and poured into them the floods.*
We can never meditate too much
*   upon your blessed person as God and as man.*
The Highest stooped to become the Lowest,
*   the Greatest took his place among the least.*

Son of Mary, you are also Son of Jehovah!
Man formed from the substance of your mother,
you are also essential deity:
we worship you this day in spirit and in truth!

We worship you because you were born of a woman,
*   wrapped in swaddling bands, laid in a manger,*
*   nursed by your mother as any other little child.*
We worship you because you grew in stature
like any other human being:
*   you ate and drank,*
*   you hungered and thirsted,*
*   you rejoiced and sorrowed.*
Your body could be touched and handled;
your body could be wounded and made to bleed.
You were no ghost but a man of flesh and blood,
*   even as we are:*
a man needing sleep,
*   a man requiring food,*
*   a man subject to pain,*
*   a man who, in the end, yielded up his life to death:*
*   a real man, a man of our race, the Son of Man.*

We worship you because you came as
a representative man, the second Adam,
sharing our flesh and blood,
making yourself of no reputation,
taking upon yourself the form of a servant,
made in the likeness of men.

It would not have been consistent with divine justice
for any other substitution to have been accepted for us
except that of a man.
Humanity sinned,
and humanity had to make reparation
for the injury done to the divine honour.
The breach of the law was caused by man,
and it had to be repaired by man.
Man had transgressed;
man had to be punished.
It was not in the power of an angel to have said,
"I will suffer for man"—
angelic sufferings would have made no amends
for human sins.
But you, the Man, the matchless Man,
being the representative Man,
our Kinsman-Redeemer, stepped in;
you suffered what was due,
you made amends to injured justice,
and by this set you us free!
Glory be to your blessed name!

As your Father saw in your humanity
a suitability to become our Redeemer,
we pray that we will see in your humanity
an attraction that leads us to approach you in faith.

Charles Spurgeon (1834-1892)[24]

SATURDAY

O SWEET EXCHANGE

"At one time we too were foolish, disobedient, deceived and enslaved by all kinds of passions and pleasures. We lived in malice and envy, being hated and hating one another. But when the kindness and love of God our Saviour appeared, he saved us, not because of righteous things we had done, but because of his mercy."
(Titus 3 v 3-5)

Titus 3 could not be more emphatic: we have no capacity to save ourselves or even to contribute to our salvation. We were not like climbers, heroically battling to the top of the mountain of divine knowledge, needing a little help to complete the final stretch. No, instead we were defiantly heading in the opposite direction. Each one of us had rejected God and become entrenched in our opposition to him. *But God,* says verse 4. God intervened. God has saved his enemies. Why? Was it because of the righteous things we had done? Was he rewarding those of us who have at least made a bit of an effort? No. It was all down to his kindness, love and mercy. His kindness "appeared" at Christmas and was displayed at Easter. Left to ourselves, human beings are foolish, disobedient and deceived. We are full of malice, envy and hatred. "But ... God" is full of kindness, love and mercy. The 2nd-century "Epistle to Diognetus" is an early example of Christian apologetics whose author is unknown to us. The writer highlights God's patience with us during our past life and the "sweet exchange" that has turned our lives around.

Oh Lord,
having planned everything with your Son,
in former times you permitted us
    to be carried away by our disordered impulses,
    to be led astray by sinful pleasures and lusts.
Not that you ever took delight in our sins,
    but you patiently bore with us;
not that you ever approved this season of iniquity,
    but because you were creating
    this present season of righteousness.
Being convinced that through our actions
    we could never attain life,
and being convinced that through our abilities
    we could never enter your kingdom,
      we have now entered
        through your power and in your kindness.
For when our iniquity had reached its height
    and it was clear that punishment and death
      were its reward,
    the season of salvation came as you ordained.

For now you have revealed
    your goodness and power,
    your boundless kindness and love.
You did not hate us;
    neither did you reject us,
    nor did you bear us malice.
Instead you were long-suffering and patient,
    and in pity you took
    the responsibility of our sins upon yourself,
    parting with your own Son so he might be our ransom:

the holy for the lawless,
  the blameless for the wicked,
    the just for the unjust,
      the incorruptible for the corruptible,
        the immortal for the mortal.
For what else but his righteousness
  could have covered our sins?
And who else but the Son of God
  could justify the lawless and ungodly?
Oh sweet exchange, oh unfathomable creation,
  oh unexpected benefits,
  that the sins of many
    should be hidden in one righteous Man,
  and the righteousness of one
    should justify many sinners!

Having in the former times
  demonstrated the inability of our nature to obtain life,
and having now revealed a Saviour
  able to save even creatures with no ability,
lead us now to trust in your kindness.
May we embrace Christ as
  our Nurse,
  our Father,
  our Teacher,
  our Counsellor,
  our Physician,
  our Wisdom,
  our Light,
  our Honour,
  our Glory,
  our Strength
  and our Life.

The Epistle to Diognetus (2nd century)[25]

The Assurance of Faith

SUNDAY

BE A JESUS TO ME

*"Kiss his son, or he will be angry and your way will lead to
your destruction, for his wrath can flare up in a moment.
Blessed are all who take refuge in him."*
(Psalm 2 v 12)

Psalm 2 describes the coming reign of God's Messiah.
God is going to restore his reign through his Son-King,
ending for ever humanity's rebellion. So the future is bleak
for rebels—and that includes every one of us. We are on a
road that leads to destruction. We are heading for the wrath
of God. And where can you hide when God is your enemy?
The answer is startling: in God himself, in the person of his
Son. Alongside this warning of judgment is an invitation to
find refuge in the Son-King, Jesus Christ. There is refuge in
Christ because he has borne the wrath of God in the place
of all those who have taken refuge in him. Anselm, the me-
dieval theologian and Archbishop of Canterbury, expresses
the horror of facing God's judgment. "Where shall I find
salvation?" he asks. The answer is Jesus, for his very name
means "Saviour" (Matthew 1 v 21).

Woe is me! Woe is me!
I have sinned. I have dishonoured God.
I have provoked the omnipotent One.
Sinner that I am, what have I done?
Against whom have I done it?

How wickedly have I done it?
Alas, alas!
Oh, wrath of the omnipotent One, do not fall on me.
Oh, wrath of the omnipotent One, how could I endure you?
There is no place anywhere in me
  that could bear your weight.
Oh, anguish!
Here, sins accusing;
there, justice terrifying;
beneath, the yawning, frightful pit of hell;
above, an angry Judge;
within, a burning conscience;
around, a flaming universe!
Where, where shall the sinner fly?
I am bound tight.
Where shall I crouch and cower?
How shall I show my face?
To hide will be impossible;
to appear will be intolerable.
I will long to hide,
but I will find nowhere to go;
I will loathe being exposed,
but everywhere I will be seen!
What then? What will happen then?
Who will snatch me from the hands of God?
Where shall I find counsel?
Where shall I find salvation?
Who is he who is called the Angel of great counsel,
who is called the Saviour,
that I may call on his name?

Here he is; here he is:
it is Jesus, Jesus himself.
Jesus the Judge, in whose hands I tremble!

Breathe again, sinner, and do not despair.
Trust in him whom you now fear.
Fly home to him from whom you have fled.
Cry to him whom you once so proudly provoked.

Jesus, Saviour, for the sake of this your name,
deal with me according to this name.
Jesus, Saviour, forget your proud provoker,
and bend your eye upon this poor invoker of your name:
 the name so sweet,
  the name so dear,
   the name so full of comfort to a sinner,
   so full of blessed hope.
For who are you, Jesus, but a Saviour?
Therefore, Jesus, for your own self's sake,
be a Jesus to me.
You who formed me, do not let me perish.
You who redeemed me, do not condemn me.
You who created me by your goodness,
 do not let your handiwork perish through my iniquity.
Kind Lord, recognise and own what is yours in me,
and take away whatever is not yours.
Jesus, Jesus, have mercy on me,
while the day of mercy lasts,
so you do not damn me on the day of judgment.
If you fold me in the wide, wide heart of your mercy,
that heart will be no less wide on my account.
Therefore admit me, O most desired Jesus;
admit me into the number of your people,
that with them I may praise you, and enjoy you,
and make my boast in you among all who love your name,
who, with the Father and the Holy Spirit,
reigns in glory throughout unending ages.

Anselm (c. 1033-1109)[26]

MONDAY

OUR COMPASSIONATE INTERCESSOR

"For we do not have a high priest who is unable to feel sympathy for our weaknesses, but we have one who has been tempted in every way, just as we are—yet he did not sin. Let us then approach God's throne of grace with confidence, so that we may receive mercy and find grace to help us in our time of need."
(Hebrews 4 v 15-16)

Yesterday the psalmist encouraged us to find refuge in Jesus (Psalm 2 v 12). But what sort of reception can we expect when we come to Jesus in faith? And what sort of reception can we expect when we come to God in prayer? One answer is sympathy. Jesus knows what it's like to be tempted, and he knows what it's like to suffer. Indeed, no one ever faced the depths of temptation he faced, nor experienced the extremity of suffering he endured. As William Symington reminds us, Jesus' experiences have equipped him to treat us with genuine, heartfelt compassion.

Second, when we come to God, we are met with grace. We come to a throne of grace, and we come through the shed blood of Christ. Whatever we may have done, God always welcomes repentant sinners. The grace of God and the sympathy of Christ add up to "confidence". We can and should come to God with confidence.

Jesus Christ, you are our compassionate Intercessor,
the Advocate who pleads our cause,
able to enter into our feelings
and make our case your own.
Your language, looks, tones and manner
melt all our doubts and hesitations.
Compassion flows not merely from your divinity
but from your humanity, with exquisite sensibility,
unaffected by the blunting influence of sin.
You plead the cause of those
whose miseries you once shared.
For of the severest afflictions,
   the bitterest temptations,
     the most pungent sorrows,
      the most awful privations,
       you had full and frequent trial.
You were not only cast into the same mould as us
   with respect to nature
but into the same furnace
   with respect to affliction.
Although you had no knowledge
of the evil of sin from personal desire,
yet well you knew its weight and its bitterness,
having had its guilt imputed to you
and its punishment exacted from you.
And now your exaltation has produced no change
in your nature or your affections.
You are the same in heaven as you were on earth:
still possessing a human nature,
still the God-Man, Emmanuel, God with us.
Human blood still flows in your veins,
and human sympathies still glow in your breast.
The compassion we feel for ourselves can never equal
   the compassion with which you regard us;

for ours is the compassion of a corrupted nature,
  but yours is the compassion of uncontaminated humanity
  indissolubly linked with all the tender mercies of deity.

Our needs never pass unnoticed.
We may miss the opportunity to bring our needs to God,
but not so our glorious Intercessor.
We can rely on you with perfect confidence:
that when we sin, you will plead for pardon;
when we are accused, you will vindicate us;
when we are afflicted, you will procure our comfort;
when we are tempted,
  you will pray that our faith does not fail;
when we perform with diligence our duties,
  you will make them acceptable with the Father.

You are no cold or selfish pleader;
your soul is in the work.
Your prayers are the prayers of the heart:
love prompts all your requests,
  selects the best arguments
      and urges the strongest pleas.
Our prayers are never as fervent as yours.

"Therefore, brothers and sisters,
since we have confidence to enter the Most Holy Place
  by the blood of Jesus,
      by a new and living way opened for us
      through the curtain, that is, his body,
and since we have a great priest over the house of God,
let us draw near to God with a sincere heart
and with the full assurance that faith brings"
(Hebrews 10 v 19-22).

William Symington (1795-1862)[27]

TUESDAY

CAST US NOT ASIDE

"All those the Father gives me will come to me, and whoever comes to me I will never drive away."
(John 6 v 37)

We often talk about how God has given Jesus to his people as a gift. (Indeed, it will be our theme next week.) But here is a truth that is perhaps just as amazing: God has given his people to Jesus as a gift! God's love-gift to his Son is you and me. A good friend of mine gave his son a remote-controlled car for Christmas, but he gave it in kit form. The two of them had to put it together before his son could enjoy the car. God the Father gave a people to Jesus. But first Jesus has had to put us together. On the cross he had to cleanse our sin and repair our brokenness. So now we are doubly precious to Jesus: as the gift of his Father and as the fruit of his suffering. No wonder he promises that he will never let us go. As the Puritan pastor John Murcot wants to impress upon us, this promise gives great reassurance to troubled Christians.

Lord Jesus Christ,
this is our comfort,
the anchor of our hearts,
the hope to which we look
in all our doubts and fears:
that you have promised never to drive us away.

May we labour to set a high price on this promise;
may we write it on our hearts in golden letters.

Lord, we confess that too often
we are prone to turn aside,
looking to broken cisterns for refreshment
    when troubles seize us.
But, alas, by their emptiness
    they quickly cause our hearts to grow dissatisfied.
We are like a bee, coming to a flower and then moving on
because it has sucked out all sweetness.
Truly, such are all things in the world
when we go to drink of them
to refresh our weary spirits.

But now we come to you to drink,
    and drink abundantly,
for in you are waters that will never fail.
No one has ever taken leave of you
because they found you empty.
No, you are a fountain full of grace,
flowing with abundant comfort.
We never need to fear
that hunger or thirst will force us away from you.

You did not drive us away
    when we first came to you;
much less will you drive us away or send us out empty
    when we come to you again
    to receive more of the fullness of your grace.
When first we came as strangers to you,
    you did not drive us away.
When first we came in a weary, burdened condition,
    you took pity on us, and gave us rest,
    welcomed us with all our sin and guilt,
    and took it away.

Will you not have an even greater heart of compassion
 for us now?
Do not cast us aside,
 despite our defects and deformities.

Lord Jesus Christ,
your tenderness towards your people
 is a feast of rich food.
Here are the aged wines
 to revive and refresh poor dropping spirits.
May we never lose the comfort of our security in you
 for lack of meditating on this.

John Murcot (1625-1654)[28]

WEDNESDAY

THE USEFULNESS OF CHRIST

"For it is we who are the circumcision, we who serve God by his Spirit, who boast in Christ Jesus, and who put no confidence in the flesh."
(Philippians 3 v 3)

What do you boast in? Your qualifications? Your wealth? Your family? Your sporting achievements or allegiances? What about before God? What is your boast before him? What gives you any sense of traction with God? Paul says that Christians put no confidence in the flesh. That basically rules out boasting in anything, anything at all, that relates to me—my achievements, efforts, understanding, background, performances, religion, morality… You get the idea! When Paul talks about "the circumcision", he's referring to those people who have had their hearts circumcised—a powerful picture of the radical inner transformation that God himself works "by his Spirit". So perhaps that is our boast? No, the whole point of this inner transformation is that it directs us away from ourselves towards Christ and to what Isaac Ambrose describes as the "infinity of worth" in his blood. So the main sign of the Spirit's transforming work is this: we boast in Christ and Christ alone. When we look within, even as Christians, we see a muddle of virtue and vice. But when we turn our eyes to Christ, we find assurance in the "infinity of worth" that resides in him.

Many are apt to lament,
  "Oh, the filth of my sins!
  Oh, the injuries I have caused
  and unkindness I have shown!
  How it troubles me that God is displeased with me."

Sweet soul! Turn your eyes to Christ.
Surely his death is more satisfactory to God
    than all your sins can possibly be displeasing to God.
There was more sweet savour in Christ's sacrifice
    than there could be offence in all your sins.
The excellence of Christ's death in making righteous
    super-abounds the filthiness of sin in making a sinner.
Come on, then,
and approach Christ with this encouragement:
there is a dignity and an excellence in this object of faith—
    Christ crucified.
There is an infinity of worth in the death of Christ.

There is an infinity of worth in the dignity of his person;
he was God-Man.
The death of angels and men, if put together,
could not have equalled the excellence of Christ's death.
The righteousness of an infinite person is now made yours;
thus it is called the "righteousness of God" (Romans 10 v 3).

There is an infinity of worth in the price offered:
it was the blood of Christ.
One drop of his blood is worth more
    than thousands of pieces of gold and silver!
This was the blood that purchased the whole church of God;
    which a thousand worlds of wealth
    could never have done (Acts 20 v 28).

Oh, the usefulness of Christ to all believing souls!
He is our life, our light,

our bread, our water, our milk, our wine.
"My flesh is real food and my blood is real drink"
(John 6 v 55).
He is our Brother, our Friend, our Husband,
He is our King, our Priest, our Prophet.
He is our justification, our sanctification,
*   our wisdom, our redemption.*
He is our peace,
*   our mediation,*
*   our atonement,*
*   our reconciliation,*
*   our all in all.*
Alas! I look on myself, and I see I am nothing;
I have nothing without Jesus Christ.
Here is a temptation; I cannot resist it.
Here is a corruption; I cannot overcome it.
Here is a persecution; I cannot endure it.
But Christ is mine:
I have an interest in Christ, a possession of Christ.
And I find enough in Christ to supply all my wants.
He was set up for this purpose:
*   to give me grace and renew my strength.*
So if I make my application to Christ,
I can suffer the loss of all things (Philippians 3 v 8);
I can do all things (Philippians 4 v 13);
I can conquer all things (Romans 8 v 37).
Oh, the joy this brings to my soul!
My soul is nothing but Christ,
and therefore I cannot but rejoice in Christ,
*   or I must rejoice in nothing at all.*
So let us "boast in Christ Jesus,
and ... put no confidence in the flesh" (Philippians 3 v 3).

Isaac Ambrose (1604-1664)[29]

THURSDAY

CORDIAL FOR A FAINTING HEART

*"Because Jesus lives for ever, he has a permanent priesthood.
Therefore he is able to save completely those who come to God
through him, because he always lives to intercede for them."*
(Hebrews 7 v 24-25)

Perhaps you can remember the excitement you felt when you first became a Christian. You came to Christ in faith and discovered the joy of knowing that your sins were forgiven. Your heart was filled with assurance and hope. But perhaps today your hope feels tarnished by your failures. Every sin chips away at your assurance. The eighteenth-century English hymnwriter Anne Steele talks about how "repeated crimes awake our fears". Take heart! The writer of Hebrews encourages us to look up to see Jesus our high priest. Because Jesus rose from the dead he is Priest for ever. And that means he ever lives to intercede for us. Every sin is covered by his blood. Every day he represents us before his Father. And Jesus is good at his job! We have no reason to fear while he is on our case. Anne Steele leads us to Jesus, our priest and advocate, in these two hymns.

Deep are the wounds which sin hath made.
Where shall the sinner find a cure?
In vain, alas, is nature's aid—
The work exceeds all nature's power.

Sin, like a raging fever, reigns
With fatal strength in every part.
The dire contagion fills the veins,
And spreads its poison to the heart.

And can no sovereign balm be found?
And is no kind physician nigh,
To ease the pain and heal the wound,
'Ere life and hope for ever fly?

There is a great physician near.
Look up, O fainting soul, and live.
See, in his heavenly smiles appear
Such ease as nature cannot give!

See in the Saviour's dying blood
Life, health, and bliss abundant flow!
'Tis only this dear sacred flood
Can cleanse the heart, and heal its woe.

Sin throws in vain its pointed dart,
For here a sovereign cure is found:
A cordial for a fainting heart,
A balm for every painful wound.

~

He lives, the great Redeemer lives.
What joy this blest assurance gives!
And now before his Father God,
Pleads the full merit of his blood.

Repeated crimes awake our fears,
And justice armed with frowns appears.
But in the Saviour's lovely face
Sweet mercy smiles, and all is peace.

Hence then, ye dark despairing thoughts,
Above our fears, above our faults,
His powerful intercessions rise
And guilt recedes, and terror dies.

In every dark distressful hour,
When sin and Satan join their power,
Let this dear hope repel the dart:
That Jesus bears us on his heart.

Great Advocate, almighty Friend—
On him our humble hopes depend.
Our cause can never, ever fail,
For Jesus pleads and must prevail.

Anne Steele (1717-1778)[30]

FRIDAY

THE FAITH-LOOK

*"We have this hope as an anchor for the soul, firm and secure.
It enters the inner sanctuary behind the curtain, where our
forerunner, Jesus, has entered on our behalf."*
(Hebrews 6 v 19-20)

An anchor fixes a boat so it cannot drift out to sea or onto the rocks. If your anchor is not secure, then your boat is not safe. The same is true for Christians. Without "an anchor for the soul" we would not be safe. But we do have an anchor. Our anchor is the promise of God. Indeed, God not only promises us salvation; he binds himself to that promise in a covenant oath. It means we can be doubly sure (Hebrews 6 v 13-18). But an anchor is only as good as the ground in which it is placed. So where is our anchor grounded? In the presence of God in heaven. That's what verse 20 means by "behind the curtain". It's an allusion to the Most Holy Place in the tabernacle, which, Hebrews 9 says, is a picture of God's sanctuary in heaven. If you're a Christian, then you're attached by an unbreakable line to heaven. It's a line that was secured for us by Jesus. He entered heaven through his blood to secure our place there. Our job is simply to trust God's promise, as today's prayer asks.

Our Father,
we wish today to come to you anew in Christ Jesus.
Many of us can look back to the happy moment

when first we saw the law fulfilled in Christ,
    wrath appeased, death destroyed,
        sin forgiven and our souls saved.
Oh, it was a happy morning—a blessed time.
Never did the sun seem to shine so brightly as then,
when we beheld the Sun of righteousness
    and basked in his light.
Many days have passed since then for some of us,
and every day we have had proofs of your faithfulness
    to the gospel of your Son.
We have proved the power of Jesus' blood
    for daily cleansing;
we have proved the power of his divine Spirit
    for daily teaching, guidance and sanctification.
And now we want no other rock to build upon
    than that upon which we have built.
We desire no other hope
    than the hope you set before us in the gospel,
    to which hope we have fled for refuge,
    and which hope we still have as an anchor of the soul,
    both sure and steadfast.

But Lord, we would begin again today
by looking to Jesus Christ anew.
Whatever our sin may be,
we desire to come to Jesus as sinners—
guilty, lost, ruined by nature—
and again to give the faith-look,
and to see him hanging on the cross for us.
We declare again that all our hope
is centred in the atoning Sacrifice
and on the risen Saviour,
who has gone into the glory
as the testimony of our justification
and of our acceptance in him.

Oh, dear Saviour, if in the course of years
we have tried to add anything to the one foundation,
if unconsciously we are relying now
upon our knowledge, our experience, our effort,
we desire to clear away all this heap of rags
and get down on the foundation again.
None but Jesus! None but Jesus!
Our souls rest in none but Jesus.
We hate and loathe with our inmost nature
the very idea of adding anything to what he has finished
or attempting to complete what is perfect in him.

Oh, this day, let your people feel
that there is now no condemnation for them.
Let them feel
    the completeness of the washing Christ has given,
        the fulness of the righteousness he has imputed,
            the eternal vitality of the life he has endowed,
                the indissoluble character of the union
                by which we are knit to Christ
                with ties that never can be broken.
May we today rejoice in Christ Jesus
and have no confidence in the flesh.
May we write upon our hearts these blessed words:
"filled [with] all the fullness of God" (Ephesians 3 v 19).
May we know that we have all that we can hold.
And may we pray to be enlarged,
    that we may take in even more of Christ
        than we have yet received.
For he is all ours, altogether ours,
    and ours world without end.

Charles Spurgeon (1834-1892)[31]

SATURDAY

WHILE CHRIST EVER LIVES

"Father, I want those you have given me to be with me where I am, and to see my glory, the glory you have given me because you loved me before the creation of the world."
(John 17 v 24)

The 19th-century Scottish pastor William Symington saw the prayers of Jesus on earth as a model of Jesus' intercession in heaven. "I have prayed for you, Simon," says Jesus in Luke 22 v 32, "that your faith may not fail". That, said Symington, is the prayer that Jesus offers in heaven on our behalf. Jesus is interceding to ensure that our faith does not fail, especially when we are under pressure. Symington applied the same logic to what is known as "the high priestly prayer" of Jesus in John 17. On earth Jesus prayed that his disciples might enjoy God's glory. In heaven Jesus continues that prayer. For those of us on earth, it is a prayer that we will remain true to Christ throughout our lives. And since Jesus makes this prayer on the basis of his shed blood, then we can be sure it will be answered.

This is why the intercession of Jesus provides assurance to troubled souls. Even once we are in heaven, our right to be there is upheld by the intercession of Jesus. His intercession is not an addition to his sacrificial death: quite the opposite. The intercession of Jesus is the application of his sacrifice.

Oh, troubled soul,
find refuge in the intercession of Christ,
which secures the complete salvation of God's chosen people,
which guarantees our entrance into heaven
    and underwrites our everlasting blessedness.
God is a rock, and his work is perfect.
What he begins, he completes;
nor will he rest until he has secured for his redeemed
    perfect acquittal beyond the reach of accusation,
        deliverance from all temptation,
            immaculate holiness,
                and uninterrupted and permanent peace.
    "Therefore he is able to save completely
    those who come to God through him,
    because he always lives to intercede for them"
    (Hebrews 7 v 25).

Oh, troubled soul,
look forward with confidence
for your reception into glory is secured
at the specific request of your Saviour:
    "Father, I want those you have given me
    to be with me where I am, and to see my glory,
    the glory you have given me because you loved me
    before the creation of the world" (John 17 v 24).
The title of your admission is his death;
but the immediate cause is his advocacy.
Your right to heaven, secured at the cross,
is carried into heaven by his intercession
and presented to God as the ground
on which your admission is to take place.

Oh, troubled soul,
fear not
for your place in glory is permanent,

sustained continually by the intercession of Jesus.
For he is "a priest for ever" (Hebrews 7 v 21).
The perpetuity of heavenly blessings
and the acceptance of celestial services
must all be traced to this source.
There is not a ray of light,
  not a smile of favour,
    not a thrill of gladness,
      not a note of joy
for which the inhabitants of heaven are not indebted
to their Mediator before the throne.
Remove this illustrious person from his situation,
  divest him of his official position,
    put out of view his priestly role,
and all the security of our heavenly benefits is gone:
the crowns fall from the heads of the redeemed,
  the palms of victory drop from their hands,
    the harps of gold are unstrung
      and the shouts of hallelujah cease for ever.
Heaven would have to expel its human inhabitants,
  sending them away into irremediable judgment!
But such an appalling catastrophe need never be feared
  while Christ ever lives to make intercession!

William Symington (1795-1862)[32]

the Gift of Christ

SUNDAY

A RICH STORE ABOUNDS IN HIM

"My goal is that they may be encouraged in heart and united in love, so that they may have the full riches of complete understanding, in order that they may know the mystery of God, namely, Christ, in whom are hidden all the treasures of wisdom and knowledge."
(Colossians 2 v 2-3)

I love any mystery story that ends with the hero finding a treasure trove, perhaps after deciphering a treasure map. Colossians 2 says that Christ is a treasure trove. In him are hidden all the blessings of God—treasures far greater than gold or silver. And there's a mystery too. But here the similarities end. For this mystery is not a puzzle to be solved but an announcement to be proclaimed: *Come and find treasure in Jesus—there's more than enough for everyone!* Or, as Paul puts it in Colossians 1 v 27, "God has chosen to make known among the Gentiles the glorious riches of this mystery, which is Christ in you, the hope of glory".

Consider today what your particular need is as you seek to live as a Christian or to serve Christ. Is there a temptation you face? Is there an opportunity before you? Are you weighed down by guilt or anxiety or shame? Are you weary in your service or distracted by the world? Do you feel unable or insecure? Do you fear the future or other people or God himself? Then use the words of John Calvin as a steer to help you see how that need is met by some aspect of the person and work of Christ.

This is the wonderful exchange which,
    out of his measureless benevolence,
    Christ has made with us:
becoming Son of Man with us,
    he has made us sons of God with him;
by his descent to earth,
    he has prepared an ascent to heaven for us;
by taking on our mortality,
    he has conferred his immortality upon us;
by accepting our weakness,
    he has strengthened us by his power;
by receiving our poverty to himself,
    he has transferred his wealth to us;
by taking the weight of our iniquity upon himself,
    he has clothed us with his righteousness.

If we seek salvation,
    we are taught by the very nature of Jesus that it is "of him".
If we seek any other gifts of the Spirit,
    they will be found in his anointing.
If we seek strength,
    it lies in his dominion;
if purity,
    in his conception;
if gentleness,
    it appears in his birth.
    For by his birth he was made like us in all respects,
    that he might learn to feel our pain.
If we seek redemption,
    it lies in his Passion;
if acquittal,
    in his condemnation;

if remission of the curse,
  in his cross;
if satisfaction,
  in his sacrifice;
if purification,
  in his blood;
if reconciliation,
  in his decent into hell;
if mortification of the flesh,
  in his tomb;
if newness of life,
  in his resurrection from death;
if immortality,
  in his resurrection to eternal life;
if inheritance of the heavenly kingdom,
  in his entrance into heaven;
if protection, security and an abundant supply of all blessings,
  in his kingdom;
if untroubled expectation of judgment,
  in the power given to him to judge.
In short, since a rich store of every kind of good
  abounds in him,
let us drink our fill from this fountain
  and from no other.

John Calvin (1509-1564)[33]

MONDAY

THE EVERY FLOWER OF LOVE

"This is love: not that we loved God, but that he loved us and sent his Son as an atoning sacrifice for our sins."
(1 John 4 v 10)

Today's prayer is adapted from a sermon by the Puritan John Flavel. Flavel says that we receive many signs of God's love every day. To be protected from danger by God's providence is a wonderful act of divine love. Food, clothes, homes, and family are all loving gifts from God. Yet when the apostle John says, "This is love", he only has one thing in mind—God sending Jesus as an atoning sacrifice. It is as if, compared to this great act of love, nothing else really counts. Flavel says, "These are great mercies in themselves; but compared to this mercy [of Christ's sacrifice], they are swallowed up, as the light of a candle when brought into the sunshine". Inside at night a candle will seem bright; but outside in the sunshine it is utterly lost in the light of the sun. In the same way, the cross outshines all of God's other gifts. The cross is the definitive demonstration of God's love for us. The circumstances of our lives may vary. We may have to go through tough times. Life may be tough for you right now. If you look at your circumstances, then you may well wonder whether God really loves you. But look at the cross. See God's love there in all its glory. And let the light of the cross outshine your doubts and fears.

Eternal Father, this is love: that you gave Christ for us.
This is the very flower of love:
you gave your precious Son to us
when you delivered him into the hands of justice
    to be punished,
as condemned persons are delivered over to the executioner,
saying,
    "All you roaring waves of my incensed justice,
    now swell as high as heaven
    and go over his soul and body;
    sink him to the bottom.
    Let him go—like Jonah, his type—into the belly of hell,
    to the roots of the mountains.
    Come, all you raging storms
    that I have reserved for the day of wrath:
    beat upon him, beat him down,
    that he may not be able to look up."

And now you give your precious Son to us again,
the application of all he purchased by his blood:
    our inheritance and portion,
    as bread to poor starving creatures,
    that by faith they might eat and live.

This gift of Christ was
the highest and fullest manifestation of your love
that ever the world saw:
    the Son of your love,
        the darling of your Soul,
            your other Self,
                yes, one with yourself,
                    the express image of your person,
                        the brightness of your glory.
In parting with him, you parted with your own heart:
a manifestation of love that will be admired to all eternity.

And you gave him up to death, even death on the cross:
  to be made a curse for us;
    to be the scorn and contempt of humanity;
      to the most unparalleled sufferings
      that ever were inflicted or borne.
You saw your Son falling to the ground,
  grovelling in the dust, sweating blood.
To wrath, to wrath,
  to the wrath of an infinite God without compromise:
  to the very torments of hell was Christ delivered.
You gave the richest jewel in your cabinet:
a mercy whose worth cannot be calculated.
Heaven itself is not as valuable and precious as Christ.
Ten thousand, thousand worlds would not be enough
to outweigh Christ's excellence, love and sweetness.
Oh, what a fair One!
What an excellent, lovely, ravishing One is Christ!
For you to bestow this mercy of mercies,
  the most precious thing in heaven or earth,
    upon poor sinners;
for you to bestow One as great,
  as lovely, as excellent as your Son was,
not upon angels, nor upon friends, but upon your enemies.
Oh, love unspeakable!

May I value the preciousness of souls as you do,
  seeing with what a high rate you value them:
  that you would give your only Son as a ransom for them.
May I value my own soul—
  not selling cheap to the temptations of sin
  what you have paid so dearly to redeem.
May I, having received the gift of your Son,
  now trust you for everything else.

John Flavel (1628–1691)[34]

TUESDAY

ALL GOODNESS

"For God was pleased to have all his fullness dwell in him, and through him to reconcile to himself all things, whether things on earth or things in heaven, by making peace through his blood, shed on the cross."
(Colossians 1 v 19-20)

All God's fullness dwells in Christ. It's an odd idea. What is God's fullness, and how can it inhabit something or someone? The answer lies in the Old Testament. In Isaiah's vision of the LORD in his temple, the angels sing, "The whole earth is full of his glory" (Isaiah 6 v 3). "Do not I fill heaven and earth?" declares the LORD in Jeremiah 23 v 24. "But will God really dwell on earth?" asks Solomon in 1 Kings 8 v 27: "The heavens, even the highest heaven, cannot contain you." God's fullness is his glorious presence everywhere. Yet even everywhere is not enough space to contain him. And yet now—wonder of wonders—all the fullness of God has been squeezed into one human person: Jesus.

And for one purpose: reconciliation. God became man so that he might make peace through his blood. The time-long hostility between God and humanity is brought to an end because Jesus has made war reparations. As man he paid what only man should pay; as God he paid what only God could afford to pay. All God's fullness has been squeezed into one human being who will give back to God the full honour that we owe—on our behalf. And so, as Catherine Parr reminds us, we long to experience more of Christ's presence because all true goodness and joy are found in him.

Lord Jesus, I pray, give me grace
to rest in you above all things,
to quiet myself in you above all creatures;
above all glory and honour,
    above all dignity and power,
        above all schemes and policies,
            above all health and beauty,
                above all riches and treasure,
                    above all joy and pleasure,
                        above all fame and praise,
                            above all mirth and consolation
                            that my heart may feel
                            apart from you.
For you, Lord God, are best:
    most wise, most high,
        most mighty, most sufficient,
            and most full of all goodness,
                most sweet, and most comforting,
                    most fair, most loving,
                        most noble, most glorious.
In you all goodness is most perfectly found.
And therefore, whatever I have apart from you,
    it is nothing compared to you.
My heart may not rest nor fully be at peace except in you.

Lord Jesus, most loving spouse,
who shall give me wings of perfect love,
    that I may fly up from worldly miseries
        and rest in you?
Oh, when shall I ascend to you,
    and feel how sweet you are?

When shall I gather myself to you so perfectly
    that I shall not, for your love, consider myself
        but only you, above myself
        and above all worldly things?
Come to me, I pray, in love.

Often I mourn the miseries of this life
    and suffer them with sorrow.
Troubles darken my thinking and hinder my thoughts,
    turning my mind from you,
    so I no longer desire you as I should,
    nor enjoy your sweet comforts,
    though they are always present for me.
I beg you, Lord Jesus,
    may the sighs of my heart move you to hear me.
O Jesus, King of everlasting glory,
    the joy and comfort of all Christian people,
    who wander as pilgrims in the wilderness of this world,
my heart cries to you in unspoken desires,
and my silence speaks to you and says,
    "How long will you wait, my Lord God, to come to me?"

Come, O Lord, and visit me,
    for without you I have no true joy;
    without you my soul is heavy and sad.
I am in prison and bound with chains of sorrow,
    until you, O Lord, with your gracious presence,
    condescend to visit me,
        to bring me again liberty and joy,
        to show your gracious face to me.
Show the greatness of your goodness,
    and let your power be glorified in me;
    for I have no other hope or refuge
    except in you and you alone, my Lord and my God.

Catherine Parr (1512-1548)[35]

WEDNESDAY

THE HISTORY OF LOVE

*"When the Lord saw her, his heart went out to her
and he said, 'Don't cry.'"*
(Luke 7 v 13)

Isaac Ambrose describes the history of Jesus as the history of love. Every incident in Christ's life, every encounter and conversation, speaks of his love. And it speaks of his love not just in the past but also of his love to you today. For Jesus has not changed. "Jesus Christ," says Hebrews 13 v 8, "is the same yesterday and today and for ever." The love of Christ we see yesterday in the four Gospels is the same love Christ feels today for you. When Jesus saw a widow burying her only son, his heart went out to her. And his heart has not changed. Today his heart goes out to you in the struggles that you face. Ambrose merges the story of Christ's life on earth with the story of Christ's work in our lives to highlight the love we have received from Christ. The aim—and let's make this our prayer today—is to fan the flames of our love for Christ.

> *Can you read the history of love—*
> *for such is the history of Christ's life—*
> *and not set on fire with love for him?*
> *Come, read again!*
> *There is nothing in Christ which is not lovely,*
> *nothing that does not win our love and draw us to him.*

When Christ saw you full of filth,
he went down into the waters of baptism,
that he might prepare a way
for the cleansing of your defiled and polluted soul.

When Christ saw the devil ready to swallow you up
and drag your soul to hell,
Christ entered the battle and overcame the devil,
that you might overcome
and triumph with Christ in his glory.

When Christ saw you, a sinner among the nations,
without God in the world,
he sent his apostles and messengers abroad
and had them preach the gospel to you.
Oh, admirable love!

When Christ saw you cast down,
he spread his arms wide to receive your soul, saying,
 "Come to me, all you who are weary and burdened,
 and I will give you rest" (Matthew 11 v 28).

When Christ saw you in suspense
and heard you wonder whether you could walk his ways,
he gave you his Spirit,
to bear the weight and make it light,
sweetening the ways of Christianity,
saying, "My yoke is easy and my burden is light"
(Matthew 11 v 30).

When Christ saw your wretched nature and pollution,
he took on your nature and took away the original sin.
When Christ saw you unclean,
a transgressor of the law in thought, word and deed,
he said to his Father on your behalf: "Here I am,
I have come to do your will" (Hebrews 10 v 9).

Oh, here is the lovely object:
  the absolute holiness and perfect purity of Christ!
This is the fairest beauty that any eye ever saw;
  this is that compendium of all glories.
How you should flame forth in love for the Lord Jesus!
Can a man stand by a hot, fiery furnace and not be warmed?
Awake, awake your ardent love towards your Lord!
Are you rock and not flesh,
that you are not wounded by these heavenly darts?
Christ loves you—is that not enough?
Christ loves you, and Christ is lovely.
His heart is set upon you,
and he is a thousand times more fair
than all the children of men.

Oh, sweet Saviour,
you say of your poor church,
even though she labours under many imperfections,
  "You have stolen my heart, my sister, my bride;
    you have stolen my heart
  with one glance of your eyes,
    with one jewel of your necklace.
  How delightful is your love, my sister, my bride!
    How much more pleasing is your love than wine,
  and the fragrance of your perfume
    more than any spice!" (Song 4 v 9-10)
Let me now say to you in return,
  "Turn your eyes to me,
  that they may overcome me:
  Let my heart be captivated.
  Let me be overcome."

Isaac Ambrose (1604-1664)[36]

THURSDAY

THE FOUNTAIN OF ALL SUPPLIES

*"It is because of him that you are in Christ Jesus, who has
become for us wisdom from God—that is, our righteousness,
holiness and redemption."*
(1 Corinthians 1 v 30)

In Colossians Paul says that "in Christ all the fullness of
the Deity lives in bodily form" (Colossians 2 v 9). All the
glory, grace, power, wisdom and love of God has, as it were,
been squeezed into the person of Christ. But then Paul
goes on: "… and in Christ you have been brought to fullness" (v 10). Christ is a storehouse of divine treasures which
have been made available to us. In 1 Corinthians 1 v 30
Paul highlights something of what this means. We can go to
Christ and receive from him the wisdom, righteousness, holiness and redemption that we need. Anne Dutton expands
this thought through a series of questions that she poses to
our souls. What are your spiritual needs today? Come to
Christ, for he is a storehouse of grace to needy sinners—
now and for ever.

> *Christ is the fountain of all supplies.*
> *You cannot need more than Christ has to give*
>   *and is willing to bestow.*
> *He will enrich you in your every time of need.*
> *All fullness dwells in Christ,*
>   *to supply us in all our emptiness.*

Do you see your nakedness?
Christ's name is "the LORD Our Righteous Saviour"
(Jeremiah 23 v 6).

Do you groan under your unholiness of heart and life?
Christ has become our sanctification,
to present defiled worms like us
perfectly holy before God.
Now he clothes us in his own personal purity,
and in the future he will maintain, increase, and perfect
that purity of heart,
which is begun in us by his Holy Spirit,
until we are perfectly conformed
to the image of Christ, our holy Head.

Does your folly,
and your inability to know the things of God
in their greatness and glory, grieve you?
Christ of God has become our wisdom.
It is his office, as our prophet,
to teach ignorant souls who come to him.
It is his joy to teach us,
and his teachings are effective
in those who humbly wait upon him.

Does your spiritual poverty distress you,
and do your spiritual enemies afflict you?
Christ has become our redemption.
And our Redeemer is great and strong.
His redemption is perfect.
Your Redeemer has paid all your debts,
and bought you and your inheritance.

Your whole person, made perfect,
shall be taken by him into his own embrace
to enjoy the most intimate communion in love, life and glory

throughout a blessed eternity!
And can your heart conceive, my dear friend,
a fraction of that bliss,
that vast inheritance of God,
which a believer has in Christ?
I tell you no!
Eye has not seen, nor ear heard,
neither has it entered into the human heart
to conceive of those great things
which God has prepared for those who love him!
(1 Corinthians 2 v 9)

Come then, my dear friend;
come by faith
and lie down by the side of Christ,
*   in his person and fullness,*
*   which are yours through infinite love.*
For this Jesus is the rest, the refreshment,
*   in which the weary soul may rest.*
The love of Christ to you and your salvation in him
are unchangeable amid all the changes of your life.
Abide in him by faith,
and cleave to him in love.

Anne Dutton (1692-1765)[37]

FRIDAY

MEDICINE FOR THE SOUL

"We have seen his glory, the glory of the one and only Son,
who came from the Father, full of grace and truth."
(John 1 v 14)

How many times have you prayed the words of "the Grace", based on 2 Corinthians 13 v 14, which begins, "May the grace of our Lord Jesus Christ..."? At my church it's often how we end our meetings. "Grace" is God's undeserved kindness. What we deserve is judgment and hell; but what we get in the gospel is forgiveness and glory. And this grace comes to us through Jesus. His death makes the blessings of grace possible. God can declare guilty people innocent because at the cross Jesus swapped places with us. He bore our punishment so we could receive his righteousness. So Jesus is not only gracious—he's *full* of grace. He is not gracious to us up to a point or only when it suits him (as we're inclined to be); he is *full* of grace. His grace took him from the heights of heaven to the depths of hell, and all to rescue sinners who had abused his love. The Puritan Thomas Watson invites us to consider the grace of Christ from every angle so we get a sense of its fullness and richness. What we discover is music to our ears, honey in the mouth and a cordial for the heart.

Why was Jesus Christ made flesh?
The primary cause was free grace.

See here, as in a mirror, the infinite love of God the Father:
when we had lost ourselves through sin,
God, in the riches of his grace, sent forth his Son,
born of a woman, to redeem us.

And behold the infinite love of Christ,
who was willing to condescend to take our flesh.
What king would wear sackcloth over his cloth of gold?
But Christ did not disdain to take our flesh.
Oh, the love of Christ!
Had Christ not been made flesh,
    we would have been made a curse.
Had he not become incarnate,
    we would have been incarcerated, forever imprisoned.

Consider from where Christ came.
He came from heaven,
and from the richest place in heaven:
his Father's bosom, that hive of sweetness.

Consider to whom Christ came. Was it to his friends?
No, he came to sinful humanity:
    to those who had defaced his image,
        to those who had abused his love,
            to those who were rebels.
Yet he came, resolving to conquer obstinacy with kindness.

Consider in what manner he came.
He came not with the majesty of a king
attended by his bodyguards.
He came in poverty:
    not like the heir of heaven
    but like one of an inferior descent.
The place he was born in was poor:
    not the royal city Jerusalem
    but Bethlehem, a poor, obscure place.

He was born in an inn,
*   a manger was his cradle,*
*   the cobwebs were his curtains,*
*   and the beasts his companions.*

Consider why he came:
that he might take our flesh to redeem us;
that he might bestow on us a kingdom.
He was poor,
*   that he might make us rich.*
He was born of a virgin,
*   that we might be born of God.*
He took our flesh,
*   that he might give us his Spirit.*
He lay in the manger,
*   that we might lie in paradise.*
He came down from heaven,
*   that he might bring us to heaven.*
And what was all this but love?
Unless our hearts are rocks,
*   this love of Christ should affect us—*
*   a love that surpasses knowledge!*

Jesus Christ has perfection in every grace.
He is a storehouse of all heavenly treasure;
*   the concentrated essence of the gospel;*
*   the wonder of angels;*
*   the joy and triumph of saints.*
The name of Christ is sweet:
*   like music to the ear,*
*   like honey in the mouth,*
*   like a cordial for the heart.*

Thomas Watson (c. 1620-1686)[38]

SATURDAY

THE ALTOGETHER LOVELY

"My beloved is radiant and ruddy, outstanding among ten thousand ... His mouth is sweetness itself; he is altogether lovely. This is my beloved, this is my friend."
(Song of Songs 5 v 10, 16)

For centuries Christians have believed that the Song of Songs pictures the love of God for his people. On the face of it, the Song tells the story of two human lovers and celebrates the joy of marital love. But there are signs that the writer intended more than this. For example, the woman is likened to the land of Israel, often in ways that don't seem to work as descriptions of human beauty. Is the bride in the Song like Israel or is Israel like a bride? It's a link that Isaiah makes when he says to the people of Israel, "Your land will be married" (Isaiah 62 v 4).

The poem is also full of garden imagery, taking us back to the Garden of Eden. Here is the restoration of the intimacy of Eden that was lost when humanity rebelled against God. What is certainly true is that all human intimacy is a picture of Christ's love for his people. Today's prayer is adapted from a letter written by the 17th-century Scottish pastor and theologian Samuel Rutherford. Echoing the language of the Song of Songs, Rutherford speaks of his longing for Christ and his longing that others would share his delight in Christ.

Precious Saviour,
  how ravishing is your beauty,
    how sweet and powerful your voice,
      the voice of that One well-beloved!
You have run away with my soul's love,
so it cannot be commanded by other lovers.
If there were ten million worlds, full of men and angels,
you would not struggle to supply our wants or fill us all.
You are a well of life,
  and who knows how deep it is to the bottom?
We cannot but love someone fair,
and, oh, what an excellent, lovely, ravishing One you are!
All the combined beauty of ten thousand paradises
compared to you, my fair and dearest Well-beloved,
would be less than one drop of rain
in all the seas of ten thousand earths.
You are the wonder of heaven and earth,
  the "altogether lovely!" (Song 5 v 16).

Oh, that I could persuade ten thousand of Adam's sons
  to flock about you, my Lord Jesus,
    and take their fill of love!
Oh, what an everlasting pity it is
  that so few take hold of you:
    so boundless, so bottomless, and so incomparable
    in your infinite excellence and sweetness.
Oh, what a pity
  that you should be so large in sweetness and worth,
  and we so pinched and empty of happiness,
  and yet people will not receive you!
Oh, that poor, dry, dead souls
  would come to this huge, fair, deep, sweet well of life,
  and fill all their empty vessels.
Alas, that Adam's foolish, wasteful heirs

lavish their affections on dead creatures and broken idols,
and do not bring their hearts to you.

But let me come near, and fill myself with you,
and satisfy my deep desires.
Too often I have a sore heart and a pained soul,
for the want of this and that idol!
Woe, woe to the mistakings of my miscarrying heart,
that gapes and cries for creatures,
and is not pained for the want of a soul's-fill of your love!
Oh, that I were chained to your love!

Oh, that you would come near, my Beloved!
Oh, my fairest One, why do you stand far away!
Come here, that I may be filled full with your excellent love.
Precious Jesus, let us meet and join together,
my soul and my Bridegroom in each other's arms.
Oh, what a meeting together this is:
to see my ugliness and your beauty,
my shame and your glory,
my baseness and your highness
kiss each other!
May I force my way
through the thorns of life
to be with you.
Do not let me lose sight of you
in this cloudy and dark day.
May I sleep with you in my heart
in the night.

Samuel Rutherford (1600-1661)[39]

The Victory of God

PALM SUNDAY

WE MAY LIFT HIM UP IN OUR HEARTS

*"The whole crowd of disciples began joyfully to praise God
in loud voices for all the miracles they had seen: 'Blessed is
the king who comes in the name of the Lord!' … Some of the
Pharisees in the crowd said to Jesus, 'Teacher, rebuke your
disciples!' 'I tell you,' he replied, 'if they keep quiet,
the stones will cry out.'"*
(Luke 19 v 37-40)

Today is Palm Sunday, when we remember how, as Jesus
entered Jerusalem, he was acclaimed by the crowds. It
was a prophetic moment—a sign of his true identity and
status. But it was not humanity's final verdict on Jesus. A
few days later the religious leaders judged Jesus to be a blasphemer; the political authorities condemned him as a rebel;
and public opinion cried out for his crucifixion. But Good
Friday was not the end of the court case. In the court of
heaven, the verdict of humanity was overturned. Jesus was
not a blasphemer—he is the Son of God. Nor was he a rebel—he is the rightful King of creation. In today's reading,
adapted from Thomas Watson, we first give assent to the
verdict of heaven as we praise the exalted Jesus. Then we
turn from praising Christ to addressing our own hearts, that
we might find comfort in Christ's exaltation.

We worship you, Lord Jesus, exalted above the heavens.
On earth you were hated and scorned by men;

now you are adored by angels.
On earth your name was reproached;
*   now God has given you*
*   "the name that is above every name" (Philippians 2 v 9).*
On earth you came in the form of a servant;
*   now the kings of the earth cast their crowns before you.*
On earth you were a man of sorrows;
*   now you are anointed with the oil of gladness.*
On earth was your crucifixion;
*   now your coronation.*
On earth your Father frowned on you in desertion;
*   now he has set you at his right hand.*
Oh, what a change!
You have been exalted at God's right hand;
the key of government is laid on your shoulders;
you govern all the affairs of the world for your own glory.

And though so highly advanced,
*   with all power in heaven and earth in your hands,*
yet still you take care of your elect people,
turning the most astonishing providences
to the good of your church.
Like a clock whose wheels move across one another,
but all make the clock strike,
so you make the most cross-providences
move towards the salvation of your church.

We worship you, Lord Jesus, seated at God's right hand,
for the work of our redemption is finished.
If you had not fully cancelled sin and satisfied God's law,
you would still be lying in the grave.
But your glory is a clear sign
that you have done and suffered all that was required
for accomplishment of our redemption.

And though so highly exalted in glory,
yet you do not forget your people on earth.
You are our high priest, with all the names and wants
of your people written upon your breastplate. Amen.

∽

This is comfort for the poorest Christian.
Are you tempted?
    Though Christ be in glory, he knows how to comfort you.
      "For we do not have a high priest who is unable
       to feel sympathy for our weaknesses" (Hebrews 4 v 15).
Do you mourn your sin?
    Christ, though in a glorified state,
    hears your sighs and bottles your tears.
Do you scarcely have a house in which to lay your head?
    You can look up to heaven, and say,
    "There is my house; there is my country.
    I have already taken possession of heaven in Christ.
    I shall sit there with him in glory; I have his word for it:
      'To the one who is victorious, I will give the right
      to sit with me on my throne'" (Revelation 3 v 21).
Just as here Christ puts his grace upon the saints,
so shortly he will put his glory upon them.
Christ's exaltation is our exaltation.
    "I have given them the glory that you gave me,
    that they may be one as we are one" (John 17 v 22).
We cannot lift up Christ higher in heaven,
but we may lift up him in our hearts.
So let us believe him, adore him and love him,
and exalt him in our lives,
for all the doxologies and prayers in the world
do not exalt Christ as much as a holy life.

Thomas Watson (c. 1620–1686)[40]

MONDAY

OUR PHOENIX RISES

"The sting of death is sin, and the power of sin is the law.
But thanks be to God! He gives us the victory through
our Lord Jesus Christ."
(1 Corinthians 15 v 56-57)

The first Easter Sunday was a day of victory and the beginning of an eternity of victory. For us that victory is
still partial. Jesus rose as the beginning of a new era, but
the old era continues and will do so until Christ returns.
So sin still can influence us, Satan can still accuse us; guilt
can still assault us, and fear still besiege us. But it is also
true that Jesus has atoned for our sin, defeated our enemy,
cleansed our guilt and assuaged our fears. So for now we live
with this tension—feeling our mortality but knowing that
immortality awaits, battling temptation but knowing that
victory is assured. Some days we will feel the struggle keenly.
But even on those days we can look up to see the resurrected
Jesus, the promise of our coming victory. For one day Jesus
will return, and his victory in our lives will be complete. Let
the words of the 17th-century pastor Thomas Adams, as he
writes of Easter Sunday, express your confidence in the victory of the resurrection and point you forward to the con-
summation of that victory when Christ returns.

Eternal Father, we praise you
for this day, the Sabbath of the new world,

our Passover from everlasting death to life,
  our true jubilee,
    the first day of our week,
      and the chief day in our calendar.
Today our Phoenix rises from his ashes,
  our Eagle renews his feathers,
    the First-begotten of the dead is born
    from the womb of the earth.
His death justified us;
  his resurrection justified his death.
His resurrection was the first stone of the foundation
  and the last stone of the roof.
Satan danced on Jesus' grave with joy,
  thinking he had Jesus entombed for ever.
But Jesus rose again
  and trampled on the devil's throne in triumph.
As you spoke to the fish,
  and it cast up Jonah,
so you commanded the earth,
  and it delivered up Jesus.

Eternal Father, we praise you,
for Christ leads us to heaven
  through the grave,
just as Moses led the people to Canaan
  through the wilderness.
Christ's resurrection is not only the object of our faith
  but the example of our hope.
The body of our Lord Jesus Christ,
  which was given for us,
  preserves our bodies and souls into everlasting life.
We all carry mortality about us,
  and the strongest man is like Nebuchadnezzar's image:
  though his head be of gold, yet his feet are of clay.

Did death kill Christ? Christ shall therefore kill death.
He who this day rose from the clods of earth
we expect one day from the clouds of heaven:
    to raise our bodies,
        to perform his promises,
            to finish our faith,
                to perfect our glory
                    and to draw us unto himself.
There shall be dry ground
    instead of this valley of tears,
a land of the living
    instead of this Golgotha of the dead,
a settled mansion
    instead of this impermanent tent.
Christ had his Easter Day by himself;
    there shall be one general Easter Day for us all,
    when the wicked shall rise to contempt
    and the faithful to an eternity of days.
Eternal Father, we praise you that on that day there shall be
    no terror to frighten us,
        no sorrow to afflict us,
            no sickness to disturb us,
                no death to dissolve us,
                    no sin to endanger for evermore.

You once said,
    "Take and eat of every tree but one."
    But man wrongly took the fruit, and ate and fell.
Now Jesus says,
    "Take and eat; this is my body,
    which is given for you."
Let us not mistake again,
    but eat and live for ever.

Thomas Adams (1583–1652)[41]

TUESDAY

RESURRECTION SWEETNESS

"No, in all these things we are more than conquerors through him who loved us. For I am convinced that neither death nor life, neither angels nor demons, neither the present nor the future, nor any powers, neither height nor depth, nor anything else in all creation, will be able to separate us from the love of God that is in Christ Jesus our Lord."
(Romans 8 v 37-39)

These words come at the end of a chapter in which the apostle Paul has described our battle with sin, our suffering as creatures in a fallen creation, and our suffering as Christians in a hostile world. He's talked about experiences of profound weakness when we hardly know how to pray (v 26). He's just been talking about trouble, hardship, persecution, nakedness, danger and sword (v 35). *Nevertheless*, he says in conclusion, *we are conquerors through him who loved us* (v 37).

Notice that it is not through him who "loves" us (present tense). Looking to our present experience of God's love would be hazardous because we might not always feel loved in the midst of suffering. We need a better foundation than our feelings. So instead Paul looks back to the cross, the supreme demonstration of God's love (5 v 8). Whatever is happening and however we feel, we see in the cross God's commitment to us. Paul also looks to the power of the resurrection (8 v 34). The cross looked like the end of the story, but then Jesus rose again. Nothing can separate us from the love of the resurrected Saviour, for death is defeated and the future is secure. God's love in Christ survived death and judgment, and so you can be sure it will survive whatever you are facing.

Today Isaac Ambrose leads our souls into the consulting room. He asks us a serious of diagnostic questions to find out what ails us before administering a dose of resurrection medicine.

> *Some people may ask, "What is the benefit to us of Christ's resurrection? What privileges flow from the power and virtue of Christ's resurrection, as well as his death?" Tell me what state you're in. Here are some of the conditions of your soul in which you may draw sweetness from Christ's resurrection.*
>
> *1. Is your conscience troubled by sin?*
> *God's word says we have "the pledge of a clear conscience toward God ... by the resurrection of Jesus Christ" (1 Peter 3 v 21).*
>
> *2. Are you afraid of condemnation?*
> *God's word says, "He was delivered over to death for our sins and was raised to life for our justification" (Romans 4 v 25).*
>
> *3. Do you question your regeneration?*
> *God's word says, "In his great mercy he has given us new birth into a living hope through the resurrection of Jesus Christ from the dead" (1 Peter 1 v 3).*
>
> *4. Are you distressed, persecuted and troubled on every side?*
> *God's word tells you where your confidence, comfort and courage now lie: namely, in the life of Christ and the resurrection of Christ. "We always carry around in our*

body the death of Jesus, so that the life of Jesus may also be revealed in our body. For we who are alive are always being given over to death for Jesus' sake, so that his life may also be revealed in our mortal body" (2 Corinthians 4 v 10-11).

5. Are you afraid of falling away?
Why, remember that the immutable force and perpetuity of the new covenant is secured by the resurrection of Jesus Christ. "I will make an everlasting covenant with you, my faithful love promised to David" (Isaiah 55 v 3). The apostle Paul applies this promise to the resurrection of Christ, as the foundation of that sure covenant: "God raised him from the dead so that he will never be subject to decay. As God has said, 'I will give you the holy and sure blessings promised to David'" (Acts 13 v 34).

6. Are you afraid of death, hell, and the power of the grave?
Why, remember that Christ is risen from the dead, and by his resurrection death is swallowed up in victory. So now you may sing, "Where, O death, is your victory? Where, O death, is your sting? … Thanks be to God! He gives us the victory through our Lord Jesus Christ" (1 Corinthians 15 v 55, 57).

Isaac Ambrose (1604-1664)[42]

WEDNESDAY

ALL THINGS APPLAUD YOU

"You will go out in joy and be led forth in peace; the mountains and hills will burst into song before you, and all the trees of the field will clap their hands."
(Isaiah 55 v 12)

The resurrection of Christ is the basis not just of the restoration of God's people but also of God's world. Creation currently groans under the curse of human sin, but one day it will be liberated and renewed along with us (Romans 8 v 19-22). Over the centuries Christians have seen spring as an annual picture of this coming joy. "The Easter Poem" of Venantius Fortunatus, a 6th-century bishop and poet, is a good example of this.

The seasons blush varied with fairer weather,
and the sky-gate opens to greater light.
The path of the fire-breathing sun rises higher,
before dipping beneath the ocean's depth.
He is armed with rays of light and warmth,
travelling and traversing the liquid elements.
Brilliant skies shine forth their countenance,
and the bright stars radiate with joy.

The earth pours out its gifts increasingly,
as the year returns its springtime wealth.
Soft beds of violets paint the plain purple;

and the herbs smile bright with their beautiful blooms.
The corn springs up far and wide in the fields,
hope for the hunger of the husbandman.
Deserting its stem, the vineshoot extends in joy,
drawing in water and giving out wine.

For in honour of Christ, rising triumphant
after descending to the gloom of death,
every grove with its leaves expresses approval;
the birds and the flowers proclaim his praise.
The light of the heavens, the fields, and the sea
worship our God, ascending to the stars.
Having crushed the laws of death and hell,
he who was crucified ascends over all.

Welcome this day, all of creation:
Jesus has conquered and gained the stars!
The changes of years and the light of days,
all things applaud you and offer their praise.
The leaves of the trees clap in excitement;
the vine, with its silent shoots, gives you its thanks.
The thickets resound with the chatter of birdsong;
every sparrow sings with exuberant love.

O Christ, you saw us plunged in our misery.
To rescue humanity you became man:
you chose human flesh, to be born and to die;
the Author of life had the rites of a funeral;
you entered the path of death for salvation,
smashing the gloomy chains of the law.
The chaos shrank from the light of your presence;
darkness has fled with the brightness of dawn.

The third day has come and you have arisen:
the promise fulfilled, your reign has begun.
It was so unfitting for your limbs to lie buried,

for worthless stones to hide the world's ransom.
It was so unworthy that a rock should confine you,
the One who encloses all things in your hands.
Cast off the linen clothes, leave them behind you:
you are enough for us; without you is nothing.

The chains of death have been released;
what sank below is recalled above.
Your face is seen that all may see light;
the day returns which fled at your death.
Return, holy Conqueror, filling the heavens!
Hell lies supressed, its rights gone for good.
Satan the spoiler has fallen prey to you,
and your people follow you, free from the grave.

Good Shepherd, enjoy your snow-white flock.
Draw wandering sheep from the beast of prey.
Those whom Adam's guilt once had poisoned,
restore and nurture within your church.
May what is sown return to you hundredfold,
filling your barns with an abundant crop.
Strengthen your people, safe in your arms:
keep us blameless and bear us to the stars.

Venantius Fortunatus (c. 530-600/609)[43]

THURSDAY

MENTAL ANGUISH

"[Jesus said,] 'Now my soul is troubled, and what shall I say?
"Father, save me from this hour"? No, it was for this very
reason I came to this hour. Father, glorify your name!'
Then a voice came from heaven, 'I have glorified it,
and will glorify it again.'"
(John 12 v 27-28)

These verses capture two amazing truths about Jesus. First, he felt real anguish as he faced the prospect of the cross. As the 5th-century church father Cyril of Alexandria highlights, this reminds us that Jesus is truly human. His humanity is not a "deceptive appearance or mere fancy". But, second, we see in these verses the resolute love of Jesus. Jesus was deeply troubled by the suffering he was about to endure, but he also recognised that this was why he came—to redeem his people in love. In John's Gospel the hour of glory is the cross (John 12 v 32-33). This was when Jesus would be literally lifted up as he was hoisted up on the cross, but it was also when he would be metaphorically lifted up as his saving love became evident and he draws all people to himself. Reflecting on John 12, Cyril reminds us that Christ's experience of suffering helps us in ours; his anguish calms our anguish and his troubled soul liberates troubled souls. We may experience a measure of this deliverance in this life—and this is our prayer today—but the fullness we will enjoy in the life to come.

My Saviour, Jesus Christ, a man born of woman,
* not in deceptive appearance or mere fancy*
* but rather by nature and in truth,*
* possessing every human quality, except for sin—*
for that which has not been taken into your nature
* has not been saved—*
you are the firstfruits of a new humanity:
in you our nature was restored to newness of life,
for you are the second Adam.

For my profit these human feelings troubled you:
in this way and no other could my healing come to pass.
As a man you felt hunger and weariness;
as a man you felt the mental anguish of suffering.
Yet you were not agitated like we are,
for the truth restored your courage.
For you, the Word of God, were made one
* with your human nature in its entirety,*
* so you might save the whole person.*

After speaking of being troubled, you did not sink into silence
but transformed the suffering which had affected you
into dauntless courage.
You despised death and the shame of suffering,
* looking only to what your suffering would achieve,*
* beholding our death in your death,*
* knowing the power of corruption would soon be destroyed,*
* seeing the transformation of human nature*
*   to newness of life for ever.*

The cross is glory.
For at the season of your Passion,
you willingly and patiently endured many insults,
and voluntarily accepted sufferings for our sake
* which you could have refused.*

Suffering like this for the benefit of others
is a sign of your boundless compassion and supreme glory.

We glorify you, too, because you overpowered death.
And so we acknowledge that you are Life,
  the Son of the living God.
And the Father is glorified
  when he is seen to have such a Son begotten of himself,
  of the same Nature as himself.
He is Good, Light, Life, and superior to death,
  the One who does whatever he will.

Just as death was reduced to nothing by your death,
and by your death alone,
so also, Christ our Saviour,
unless you had felt dread,
  human nature could not have become free from dread;
unless you had experienced grief,
  there could never have been any deliverance from grief;
unless you had been troubled and alarmed,
  no escape from these feelings could have been found.

With every affection to which human nature is liable,
we find the corresponding affection in Christ.
The affections of your flesh were aroused,
not that they might have the upper hand as they do in us,
but in order that they might be thoroughly subdued
by the power of the Word dwelling in the flesh,
the nature of humanity thus being changed for good.

So now when we feel overwhelmed
  by dread or grief or alarm,
restore our courage with the truth of the word,
and comfort our hearts through the Word made flesh.

Cyril of Alexandria (c. 376-444)[44]

GOOD FRIDAY

OUR GREATEST GLORY

*"For the message of the cross is foolishness to those
who are perishing, but to us who are being saved it is
the power of God."
(1 Corinthians 1 v 18)*

From the earliest days people have regarded faith in a crucified Saviour as foolish. It's not hard to see why. How can a man dying on a Roman cross be the power of God? If anything, it looks like the epitome of weakness and failure. But the 4th-century bishop Cyril of Jerusalem invites us to glory in the cross. The miracles of Jesus look impressive, but they are nothing compared to the cross, however counterintuitive that feels. That's because the cross atones for the sin of God's people across the ages and throughout the world. God, says Cyril, could have been true to his justice and destroyed humanity. But what then of his loving-kindness? Or God could have overlooked sin. But what then of his justice? The glory of the cross is that God forgives our sin while remaining true to his justice. For Christ "took our sins" and the penalty they demand on himself at the cross. And Jesus was not simply a man, but the God-Man with life in himself. So his death brings life to all those who are his. This is our glory this Good Friday.

*Everything you did, Lord Jesus, gives us reason to glory.
But our greatest glory of all is your cross:*

"May I never boast
except in the cross of our Lord Jesus Christ"
(Galatians 6 v 14).
It was truly wonderful that one blind from birth
should receive sight in Siloam (John 9 v 1-7).
> *But what is this compared with the blind*
> *of the whole world?*
It was a great thing, and beyond natural explanation,
for Lazarus to rise again on the fourth day (John 11 v 44).
> *But what is this compared with the dead in sins*
> *throughout the world?*
It was marvellous that five loaves
should pour forth food for the five thousand (John 6 v 1-13).
> *But what is that compared to those*
> *who are famishing in ignorance through all the world?*
It was marvellous that a woman should be set free
who had been bound by Satan 18 years (Luke 13 v 10-13).
> *But what is this compared to all of us,*
> *who were fast bound in the chains of our sins?*
The glory of your cross
> *led those who were blind through ignorance into light,*
> > *released all who were held fast by sin,*
> > > *and ransomed the whole world of mankind.*
If, because of the fruit of the tree,
we were cast out of paradise,
> *shall not believers now more easily enter into paradise*
> *because of the tree on which you died?*
If the first man formed out of the earth
brought universal death,
> *shall not you, who formed him out of the earth,*
> *bring eternal life, being yourself the Life?*
If Phineas, when he waxed zealous and slayed the evildoer,
halted the wrath of God (Numbers 25),
> *shall not you, Jesus, who did not slay another*

but gave up yourself for a ransom,
put away the wrath which is against mankind?

May we never be ashamed of the cross of our Saviour
but rather glory in it.
For it was not a mere man who died for us,
for you are the Son of God: God made man.
If the Passover lamb drove the destroyer away,
* how much more will you, the Lamb of God,*
* who takes away the sin of the world,*
* deliver us from our sins?*
If the blood of a foolish sheep gave salvation,
* shall not the blood of the Only-begotten much rather save?*

All these things you endured,
and made peace through the blood of your cross.
For we were enemies of God through sin,
and God had appointed the sinner to die.
It seemed that one of two things must happen:
either God in his truth should judge all humanity
or God in his loving-kindness should cancel the sentence.
But behold the wisdom of God:
he preserved both the truth of his sentence
and the exercise of his loving-kindness.
For you took our sins in your body on the tree,
* that we by your death might die to sin*
* and live to righteousness.*
The transgression of sinners was not as great
* as your righteousness;*
the sin which we committed was not so great
* as the righteousness you accomplished*
* when you laid down your life for us.*

Cyril of Jerusalem (c. 313-386)[45]

HOLY SATURDAY

CONQUERING LOVE

*"Therefore I will give him a portion among the great, and he
will divide the spoils with the strong, because he poured out
his life unto death, and was numbered with the transgressors.
For he bore the sin of many, and made intercession for
the transgressors."*
(Isaiah 53 v 12)

A more literal translation of this verse is this: "I will allocate many as an allocation to him, and he will allocate
the strong as plunder". In other words, we are the reward that
God gives to his Son. Jesus has obeyed his Father, even though
this meant dying on the cross. His reward is to be given us as
his people. Jesus associated himself with us for he "was numbered with the transgressors". He bore our sin so we would be
redeemed. His reward is the salvation of his people. He shares
the spoils of his victory with us—with you. In today's prayer,
Charles Spurgeon leads us in submitting to Christ's conquer-
ing love—loving him as his love deserves and letting him take
possession of the lives he has won.

Gracious God, we praise you with our whole hearts
  for the wondrous revelation of your love
  in Christ Jesus our Lord.
We think every day of his Passion,
  for all our hope lies in his death.
But as often as we think upon it,

we are still filled with astonishment
    that you should so love the world
    as to give your only begotten Son,
    that whoever believes in him should not perish
    but have everlasting life (John 3 v 16).
We are astonished that heaven's eternal darling
should come to earth to be made man,
and in manhood's form be despised and rejected
by the very people whom he came to bless,
and then should bear the sin of many
    and be numbered with the transgressors,
        and die a transgressor's death,
            a felon's death, upon the gibbet of the cross.
Oh, this would surpass all belief
    if it had not actually been so.
It would have seemed blasphemy to suggest such a thought,
    yet you have done it.
Your grace has almost out-graced itself;
your love has reached its height:
    love to rebels,
    love that meant even your Son could not be spared.
Oh God, we are afflicted in our hearts
to think we do not love you more after such love as this.
We lie in the dust before you in utter shame,
    for we have sometimes heard this story without emotion
    and told it without tenderness.
Yet the theme has never become stale to us.
The story of Christ's death still brings us joy
    and makes our hearts leap.
And yet, Lord, it does not move us as much as it should.
Give us more tenderness of heart.
Give us to feel the wounds of Jesus
    until they wound our sins to death.
Give us to have a heart pierced as his was

with an all-consuming love for his blessed Person.
We adore you, Father,
*   for your great love in the gift of Jesus.*
We adore you, most blessed Jesus,
*   for resigning your life for our sakes.*
We adore the blessed Spirit
*   for you have led us to know this mystery*
*   and to put our trust in Jesus.*

And now we pray to you, great God, that in us
your dear Son may see the fruit of the pains of his soul.
Lord, let him see a reward for his sufferings
*   in all of us being repentant for sin,*
*   trusting in God*
*   and confessing his name.*

Oh, Lord and Master, Redeemer and Saviour,
come and take entire possession of us.
By force of arms, the arms of love,
*   will you capture our wilful, wayward spirits.*
Come and divide the spoil with the strong in us we pray.
Take every faculty and use it;
*   overpower and sanctify it.*
Help us employ every moment of our time for you,
and breathe every breath out to your honour.
We confess there is still unconquered territory in our lives.
Subdue, Lord, we beg you, our corruptions;
cast them out, and in our spirit rule and conquer.
There set up your eternal throne.

Charles Spurgeon (1834-1892)[46]

EASTER SUNDAY

TO WAKE MORE MERRY

*"I delight greatly in the LORD; my soul rejoices in my God.
For he has clothed me with garments of salvation and arrayed
me in a robe of his righteousness, as a bridegroom adorns his
head like a priest, and as a bride adorns herself with
her jewels."
(Isaiah 61 v 10)*

"We had hoped..." say the two disciples on the
road to Emmaus on the evening of that first
Easter Sunday (Luke 24 v 21). They had hoped that Jesus was God's promised messianic King. It had looked that
way for a while. But now he was dead, and it seemed that
hope had died with him. But in fact hope (in the person of
Jesus) was walking along the road with them. For Jesus had
risen! And so everything has changed. God's wrath against
our sin has been atoned for. Judgment and the curse are no
longer our future. As the 4th-century church father Gregory of Nyssa reminds us, Christ has taken off our pathetic
fig-leaf covering and instead has clothed us with garments
of salvation. Death itself has been defeated. And so, as the
17th-century Welsh poet Henry Vaughan says, graves have
become beds, and death has become a nap from which we
will "wake more merry".

*For truly you, O Lord,
are the pure and eternal fount of goodness.*

Once you justly turned away from us,
 and now in loving-kindness
  you have had mercy upon us.
Once you hated,
 and now you are reconciled.
Once you cursed,
 and now you bless.
Once you banished us from paradise,
 and now you have recalled us.
You have stripped off our unseemly fig-leaf covering
 and put on us a costly garment.
You have opened the prison
 and released the condemned;
You have sprinkled us with clean water
 and cleansed us from our filthiness.

No longer shall Adam be confounded when you call,
 nor hide himself, convicted by his conscience,
  cowering in the thicket of paradise.
Nor shall the flaming sword encircle paradise around,
 and make the entrance inaccessible
  to those who draw near.
For all is turned to joy for us,
 who once were the heirs of sin.
Paradise, yes, heaven itself may be trodden by humanity;
 and all creation, in the world and above the world,
  that once was at variance with itself,
   is knit together in friendship.
We human beings can join the angels' song,
offering the worship of their praise to you.
For all these things, then, let us sing to you that hymn of joy,
as lips touched by the Spirit long ago loudly sang:
 "I delight greatly in the LORD,
  my soul rejoices in my God.

For he has clothed me with garments of salvation
and arrayed me in a robe of his righteousness,
as a bridegroom adorns his head like a priest,
and as a bride adorns herself with her jewels"
(Isaiah 61 v 10).
Truly the Adorner of the bride is Christ,
who is, and was, and shall be
blessed now and for evermore.

Gregory of Nyssa (c. 335 – c. 395)[47]

∽

Easter Hymn
Death and darkness, get you packing,
Nothing now to man is lacking,
All your triumphs now are ended,
And what Adam marred is mended.
Graves are beds now for the weary,
Death a nap, to wake more merry;
Youth now, full of pious duty,
Seeks in thee for perfect beauty;
The weak and aged, tired with length
Of days, from thee look for new strength;
And infants with thy pangs contest
As pleasant, as if with the breast.
Then, unto him, who thus hath thrown
Even to contempt thy kingdom down,
And by his blood did us advance
Unto his own inheritance,
To him be glory, power, praise,
From this, unto the last of days!

Henry Vaughan (1621-1695)[48]

ENDNOTES

1 Ash Wednesday. Thomas Becon, *Prayers and Others Pieces* (Parker Society, 1846), p 16.

2 Thursday. Catherine Parr, "The Lamentations of a Sinner", *The Writings of Edward VI and His Reign* (Religious Tract Society, 1831), p 32-36, 38-39.

3 Friday. Abridged from Martin Luther, "How to Contemplate Christ's Holy Sufferings" (1519), *The Complete Sermons of Martin Luther, Vol. 2* (Baker, 2000), p 183-192.

4 Saturday. C.H. Spurgeon, *C.H. Spurgeon's Prayers* (Passmore & Alabaster, 1905), p 25-31.

5 Week 1 Sunday. Isaac Ambrose, *Looking Unto Jesus* (1658) (Sprinkle Publications, 1986), p 404-405, 664.

6 Week 1 Monday. Gregory of Nazianzus, "The Third Theological Oration: On the Son", *The Nicene and Post-Nicene Fathers: Second Series, Vol. 7*, eds. P. Schaff & H. Wace (Hendrickson, 1994), p 308-309.

7 Week 1 Tuesday. Stephen Charnock, "A Discourse of the Knowledge of Christ Crucified", *Works, Vol. 4* (Banner of Truth, 1985), p 503-506.

8 Week 1 Wednesday. Adapted from Anne Dutton, *Selected Spiritual Writings of Anne Dutton Vol. 1*, ed. JoAnn Ford Watson (Mercer University Press, 2003), p 192.

9 Week 1 Thursday. Augustine, *Confessions 10.69-70*, *The Nicene and Post-Nicene Fathers: First Series, Vol. 1*, ed. P. Schaff (Hendrickson, 1994), p 162.

10 Week 1 Friday. C.H. Spurgeon, *Morning and Evening*, March 28 Morning.

11 Week 1 Saturday. Isaac Ambrose, *Looking Unto Jesus (1658)*, p 597.

12 Week 2 Sunday. George Herbert, *The Complete English Works* (Everyman, 1995), p 34, 184.

13 Week 2 Monday. William Symington, *On the Atonement and Intercession of Jesus Christ*, 1834 (Reformation Heritage Books, 2006), p 265-266, 278, 268.

14 Week 2 Tuesday. James Janeway, *Heaven on Earth* (Thomas Nelson, 1847), p 157-159.

15 Week 2 Wednesday. James Janeway, *Heaven on Earth*, p 159-161.

16 Week 2 Thursday. John Owen, "Communion with God" (1657), *Works, Vol. 2* (Banner of Truth, 1966), p 61-62.

17 Week 2 Friday. C.H. Spurgeon, "A Man of Sorrows," *Sermons Vol. 19*, #1099.

18 Week 2 Saturday. William Symington, *On the Atonement and Intercession of Jesus Christ*, p 280-282.

19 Week 3 Sunday. Cyprian, "On the Advantage of Patience §7-9", *The Ante-Nicene Fathers, Vol. 5*, eds. A. Roberts & J. Donaldson (Eerdmans, 1979), p 486.

20 Week 3 Monday. Martin Luther, *A Commentary of Saint Paul's Epistle to the Galatians* (1535) (John Highlands, 1891), comments on Galatians 3 v 9; 1 v 4; 3 v 13; p 241, 46-47, 277-278, 287.

21 Week 3 Tuesday. John Bunyan, "Light for Them that Sit in Darkness" and "The Greatness of the Soul", *Works*, Vol. 1 (Banner of Truth, 1991), p 432, 131.

22 Week 2 Wednesday. Gregory of Nazianzus, "Oration 1: On Easter and His Reluctance", *The Nicene and Post-Nicene Fathers: Second Series, Vol. 7*, eds. P. Schaff & H. Wace (Hendrickson, 1994), p 203-204.

23 Week 3 Thursday. John Calvin, *Calvin: Commentaries, Library of Christian Classics*, trans. & ed. J. Haroutunian (SCM, 1958), p 69-70.

24 Week 3 Friday. C.H. Spurgeon, "A Man of Sorrows", *Sermons Vol. 19*, #1099.

25 Week 3 Saturday. "The Epistle to Diognetus", *The Ante-Nicene Fathers, Vol. 1,* eds. A. Roberts & J. Donaldson (Eerdmans, 1979), p 28.

26 Week 4 Sunday. Anselm, "A Meditation to Stir up Fear", *St. Anselm's Prayers and Meditations* (Burns & Oates, 1872), p 41-43.

27 Week 2 Monday. William Symington, *On the Atonement and Intercession of Jesus Christ*, p 286-290.

28 Week 4 Tuesday. John Murcot, "Christ's Willingness to Receive Humble Sinners: A Sermon on John 6:37", cited in C.S. Farmer (ed.), John 1-12, *Reformation Commentary on Scripture: New Testament IV* (InterVarsity, 2014), p 224-225.

29 Week 4 Wednesday. Adapted from Isaac Ambrose, *Looking Unto Jesus* (1658), p 397, 396, 313.

30 Week 4 Thursday. Anne Steele, "Deep Are the Wounds" and "He Lives, the Great Redeemer Lives", Public Domain.

31 Week 4 Friday. Adapted from C.H. Spurgeon, "The Life Look", *Pastor in Prayer* (Banner of Truth), p 89.

32 Week 4 Saturday. William Symington, *On the Atonement and Intercession of Jesus Christ*, p 282-283.

33 Week 5 Sunday. John Calvin, *Institutes*, 4.17.2 and 2.16.19.

34 Week 5 Monday. John Flavel, "Christ the Fountain of Life", *Works, Vol. 1* (Banner of Truth, 1968), p 64-69.

35 Week 5 Tuesday. Catherine Parr, "Prayers", *The Writings of Edward VI and His Reign*, p 18-19, 21.

36 Week 5 Wednesday. Isaac Ambrose, *Looking Unto Jesus* (1658), p 308-310.

37 Week 5 Thursday. Anne Dutton, *Letters on Spiritual Subjects, Vol. VI* (J. Hart, 1748), p 34-36.

38 Week 5 Friday. Thomas Watson, *The Body of Divinity* (1692) (Banner of Truth, 1965), p 194-195, 161, 164.

39 Week 5 Saturday. Samuel Rutherford, "To Lady Kilconquhar", August 8, 1637, *Letters of Samuel Rutherford: A Selection* (Banner of Truth, 1973), p 118-123.

40 Palm Sunday. Thomas Watson, *The Body of Divinity* (1692), p 206-208.

41 Holy Week Monday. Thomas Adams, Entry #1777 in *A Homiletic Encyclopaedia*, ed. R. A. Bertram (Fink & Wagnalls, 1889), p 310.

42 Holy Week Tuesday. Isaac Ambrose, *Looking Unto Jesus* (1658), p 480-481.

43 Holy Week Wednesday. Venantius Fortunatus, "The Easter Poem", *The Ante-Nicene Fathers*, Vol. 7, eds. A. Roberts & J. Donaldson (Eerdmans, 1979), p 329-330.

44 Holy Week Thursday. Cyril of Alexandria, comments on John 12:27-27, *Commentary on the Gospel According to Saint John, Vol. 2* (Walter Smith, 1885), p 150-154.

45 Good Friday. Cyril of Jerusalem, "Catechetical Lectures," 13.1-3, 33, *The Nicene and Post-Nicene Fathers: Second Series, Vol. 2.7,* eds. Philip Schaff & Henry Wace, 1886-1900, reproduced Peabody, Ma (Hendrickson, 1994), p 82, 91.

46 Holy Saturday. C.H. Spurgeon, *The Pastor in Prayer* (Banner of Truth, 2004), p 7-10.

47 Easter Sunday. Gregory of Nyssa, "On the Baptism of Christ", *The Nicene and Post-Nicene Fathers: Second Series*, Vol. 5, p 520.

48 Easter Sunday. Henry Vaughan, "Easter Hymn", in *The Soul in Paraphrase: A Treasury of Classic Devotional Poems*, ed. Leland Ryken (Crossway, 2018), p 145.

the good book

COMPANY

BIBLICAL | RELEVANT | ACCESSIBLE

At The Good Book Company, we are dedicated to helping Christians and local churches grow. We believe that God's growth process always starts with hearing clearly what he has said to us through his timeless word—the Bible.

Ever since we opened our doors in 1991, we have been striving to produce Bible-based resources that bring glory to God. We have grown to become an international provider of user-friendly resources to the Christian community, with believers of all backgrounds and denominations using our books, Bible studies, devotionals, evangelistic resources, and DVD-based courses.

We want to equip ordinary Christians to live for Christ day by day, and churches to grow in their knowledge of God, their love for one another, and the effectiveness of their outreach.

Call us for a discussion of your needs or visit one of our local websites for more information on the resources and services we provide.

Your friends at The Good Book Company

thegoodbook.com | thegoodbook.co.uk
thegoodbook.com.au | thegoodbook.co.nz
thegoodbook.co.in